Igor Stravinsky
The Rake's Progress

PAUL GRIFFITHS

with Igor Stravinsky, Robert Craft and Gabriel Josipovici

CAMBRIDGE UNIVERSITY PRESS

Cambridge
London   New York   New Rochelle
Melbourne   Sydney

Published by the Press Syndicate of the University of Cambridge
The Pitt Building, Trumpington Street, Cambridge CB2 1RP
32 East 57th Street, New York, NY 10022, USA
296 Beaconsfield Parade, Middle Park, Melbourne 3206, Australia

© Cambridge University Press 1982

First published 1982

Library of Congress catalogue card number: 81-17071

British Library Cataloguing in Publication Data
Griffiths, Paul
Igor Stravinsky: The rake's progress. –
(Cambridge opera handbooks)
1. Stravinsky, Igor. Rake's Progress.
I. Title
782.1'092'4   ML410.S932

ISBN 0 521 23746 7 hard covers
ISBN 0 521 28199 7 paperback

Transferred to digital printing 2001

Cambridge Opera Handbooks

Igor Stravinsky
The Rake's Progress

Venice 1951: Act I scene 1, with Rafael Arié as Trulove, Elisabeth Schwarzkopf as Anne, Robert Rounseville as Tom and Otakar Kraus as Shadow.

CAMBRIDGE OPERA HANDBOOKS

General preface

This a series of studies of individual operas, written for the serious opera-goer or record-collector as well as the student or scholar. Each volume has three main concerns. The first is historical: to describe the genesis of the work, its sources or its relation to literary prototypes, the collaboration between librettist and composer, and the first performance and subsequent stage history. This history is itself a record of changing attitudes towards the work, and an index of general changes of taste. The second is analytical and is grounded in a very full synopsis which considers the opera as a structure of musical and dramatic effects. In most volumes there is also a musical analysis of a section of the score, showing how the music serves or makes the drama. The analysis, like the history, naturally raises questions of interpretation, and the third concern of each volume is to show how critical writing about an opera, like production and performance, can direct or distort appreciation of its structural elements. Some conflict of interpretation is an inevitable part of this account; editors of the handbooks reflect this – by citing classic statements, by commissioning new essays, by taking up their own critical position. A final section gives a select bibliography, a discography and guides to other sources.

In working out plans for these volumes, the Cambridge University Press was responding to an initial stimulus from staff of the English National Opera. Particular thanks are due to Mr Edmund Tracey and Mr Nicholas John for help, advice and suggestions.

Books published

Richard Wagner: *Parsifal* by Lucy Beckett
C. W. von Gluck: *Orfeo* by Patricia Howard
W. A. Mozart: *Don Giovanni* by Julian Rushton
Leoš Janáček: *Káťa Kabanová* by John Tyrrell

Other volumes in preparation

IN MEMORY OF BILL HOPKINS

Contents

General preface	*page*	v
List of illustrations		xi
Acknowledgements		xiii
Dramatis personae		1
1 The composer's view *by Igor Stravinsky*		2
2 The makers and their work		5
3 A note on the sketches and the two versions of the libretto *by Robert Craft*		18
4 Synopsis		31
5 Performance history		48
6 Some thoughts on the libretto *by Gabriel Josipovici*		60
7 In an operatic graveyard: Act III scene 2		75
8 Progress and return		92
Notes		101
Bibliography		104
Discography *by Malcolm Walker*		106
Index		107

Illustrations

	Venice 1951: Act I scene 1	*frontispiece*
1	Venice 1951: the Graveyard scene	*page* x
2	Hogarth: 'The Orgy' from *The Rake's Progress* (1732–3)	9
3	Hogarth: 'The Madhouse' from *The Rake's Progress* (1732–3)	11
4	Sketch of the beginning of Act I scene 1	21
5	Sketch from Shadow's monologue in Act I scene 1	22
6	Sketch from Anne's aria in Act I scene 3	23
7	Sketch from Tom's accompanied recitative in Act II scene 1	24
8	Sketch from Tom's dialogue with the Madmen in Act III scene 3	25
9	Sketch from Tom's arioso in Act III scene 3	26
10	Stockholm 1961: the Brothel scene	52
11	Stockholm 1961: the Auction scene	53
12	Sadler's Wells 1962: the Brothel scene, with Alexander Young as Tom	55
13	Glyndebourne 1975: the Auction scene	58
14	Covent Garden 1979: the Auction scene	59

Acknowledgements

Music examples and extracts from the libretto of *The Rake's Progress* are © Copyright 1951 by Boosey & Hawkes, Inc. Reprinted by permission of Boosey & Hawkes Music Publishers Ltd.

Music examples from *The Nightingale* are © Copyright 1914 by Edition Russe de Musique. Copyright assigned 1947 to Boosey & Hawkes, Inc. for all countries. Reprinted by permission of Boosey and Hawkes Music Publishers Ltd.

'The composer's view' and 'A tribute to a librettist' are reproduced from *Themes and Episodes*, by Igor Stravinsky and Robert Craft (New York, Knopf, 1966), pp. 48–51 and 96–7 respectively. Copyright © 1966 by Robert Craft and Igor Stravinsky. Reprinted by permission of Alfred A. Knopf, Inc. They were subsequently reprinted in *Themes and Conclusions* (London, Faber, 1972), pp. 53-5 and 77 respectively. Reprinted by permission of Faber and Faber Ltd from *Themes and Conclusions* by Igor Stravinsky and Robert Craft.

The essay by Gabriel Josipovici in Chapter 6 was first published in *Tempo*, 113 (June 1975) 2-13. It then appeared in Josipovici's *Lessons of Modernism* (London and Basingstoke, Macmillan, and Totowa, New Jersey, Rowman & Littlefield, 1977) and is reprinted here by permission of those publishers.

Quotations from early versions of the libretto are copyright © 1982 by the estate of W. H. Auden. Permission to reproduce photographs was courteously granted by the Teatro alla Scala, Milan (frontispiece and Plate 1), Trustees of Sir John Soane's Museum, London (Plates 2–3), the Royal Theatre, Stockholm (Plates 10–11), Sadler's Wells Theatre (Plate 12, photograph by Reg Wilson), Glyndebourne Festival Opera (Plate 13, photograph by Guy Gravett) and the Royal Opera House, Covent Garden (Plate 14, photograph by Reg Wilson). Photographic negatives for Plates 4–9 were generously provided by the Stravinsky Estate.

1 Venice 1951: the Graveyard scene

Dramatis personae

Trulove	*Bass*
Anne, his daughter	*Soprano*
Tom Rakewell	*Tenor*
Nick Shadow	*Baritone*
Mother Goose	*Mezzo-Soprano*
Baba the Turk	*Mezzo-Soprano*
Sellem, auctioneer	*Tenor*
Keeper of the Madhouse	*Bass*

SATB chorus of whores, roaring boys, servants, citizens and madmen

Orchestra: two flutes (second doubling piccolo)
          two oboes (second doubling cor anglais)
          two B flat clarinets
          two bassoons
          two horns
          two B flat trumpets
          timpani
          harpsichord (or piano)
          strings

The action takes place in eighteenth-century England

1 *The composer's view*
BY IGOR STRAVINSKY

I. A programme note

Rather than seek musical forms symbolically expressive of the dramatic content (as in the Daedalian examples of Alban Berg), I chose to cast *The Rake* in the mould of an eighteenth-century 'number' opera, one in which the dramatic progress depends on the succession of separate pieces — recitatives and arias, duets, trios, choruses, instrumental interludes. In the earlier scenes the mould is to some extent pre-Gluck in that it tends to crowd the story into the secco recitatives, reserving the arias for the reflective poetry, but then, as the opera warms up, the story is told, enacted, contained almost entirely in song — as distinguished from so-called speech-song, and Wagnerian continuous melody, which consists, in effect, of orchestral commentary enveloping continuous recitative.

Having chosen a period-piece subject, I decided — naturally, as it seemed to me — to assume the conventions of the period as well. *The Rake's Progress* is a conventional opera, therefore, but with the difference that these particular conventions were adjudged by all respectable (i.e. progressive) circles to be long since dead. My plan of revival did not include updating or modernising, however — which would have been self-contradictory, in any case — and it follows that I had no ambitions as a reformer, at least not in the line of a Gluck, a Wagner or a Berg. In fact, these great progressivists sought to abolish or transform the very clichés I had tried to re-establish, though my restitutions were by no means intended to supersede their now conventionalised reforms (i.e. the leitmotif systems of Wagner and Berg).

Can a composer re-use the past and at the same time move in a forward direction? Regardless of the answer (which is 'yes'), this academic question did not trouble me during the composition, nor will I argue it now, though the supposed backward step of *The Rake* has taken on a radically forward-looking complexion when I have compared it with some more recent progressive operas. Instead, I ask the listener to sus-

The composer's view

pend the question as I did while composing, and, difficult as the request may be, to try to discover the opera's own qualities. For a long time *The Rake* seemed to have been created for no other purpose than journalistic debates concerning: (a) the historical validity of the approach; and (b) the question of pastiche. If the opera contains imitations, however — especially of Mozart, as has been said — I will gladly allow the charge if I may thereby release people from the argument and bring them to the music.

The Rake's Progress is simple to perform musically, but difficult to realise on the stage. I contend, however, that the chief obstacles to a convincing visual conception are no more than the result of an incapacity to accept the work for what it is. True, Tom's machine-baked bread may be hard to swallow, but even *it* will go down, I think (with a lot of butter and more than a few grains of salt) if the stage director has not lost sight of the opera's 'moral fable' proposition by over-playing the realism of 'the Rakewell story'. As Dr Johnson said, 'Opera is an exotic and irrational art.'

It is easy to find faults of this sort in *The Rake*, to be sure, though, alas, it offers nothing quite so foolish as the concealed-identity scene in *Un ballo in maschera*, or the post-stabbing coloratura concert in *Rigoletto*, to name two far greater operas which, like my own, I love beyond the point where criticism can make a difference. Having perfect 20–20 hindsight, like most people, I am now able to see that Shadow is a preacher as well as a Devil; that the Epilogue is much too 'nifty' (as Americans say); that the ostinato accompaniment style could do with an occasional contrast of polyphony, the dramatic opportunity for which might have been found in an extra ensemble or two during which the minor characters might also have been given more development and connection. But though such things matter, they are not fatal. And in any case, I am not concerned with the future of my opera. I ask for it only a measure of present justice.

Paris, 16 August 1964

II. A tribute to a librettist

I chose Wystan Auden as librettist for my opera *The Rake's Progress* because of his special gift for versification; I have never been able to compose music to prose, even poetic prose. That he was a great poet others had assured me — I felt as much, but was too new to English to judge for myself — yet my first requisite was more modest and more specific; after all, successful collaborations between musicians and poets in dramatic works have been rare, and in fact Dryden and Purcell, Hofmannsthal and Strauss, Boito and Verdi (Boito was, rather, a great adapter, but that is almost as valuable), are the only names that come to mind. What I required was a versifier with whom I could collaborate in writing songs, an unusual starting point for an opera, I hardly need to add, as most composers begin with a search for qualities of dramatic construction and dramatic sensation. I had no knowledge of Wystan's dramatic gifts or even whether he was sensible to operatic stagecraft. I simply gave all priority to verse, hoping that we could evolve the theatrical form together and that it would inspire Wystan to dramatic poetry.

I think he *was* inspired, and in any case he inspired me. At the business level of the collaboration he wrote 'words for music', and I wonder whether any poet since the Elizabethans has made a composer such a beautiful gift of them as the 'Lanterloo' dance in our opera. Wystan had a genius for operatic wording. His lines were always the right length for singing and his words the right ones to sustain musical emphasis. A musical speed was generally suggested by the character and succession of the words, but it was only a useful indication, never a limitation. Best of all for a composer, the rhythmic values of the verse could be altered in singing without destroying the verse. At least, Wystan has never complained. At a different level, as soon as we began to work together I discovered that we shared the same views not only about opera, but also on the nature of the Beautiful and the Good. Thus, our opera is indeed, and in the highest sense, a collaboration.

Wystan has lived in Austria too long now, and I wish you could convince him to come back. After all, we cannot afford to give our best poet to the Germans.

For a BBC television documentary on Auden. Hollywood, 5 November 1965.

2 The makers and their work

It is the pattern of opera that its composers should either be constantly involved with it, as Mozart, Wagner, Strauss and the Italians were, or else confine themselves to a single masterpiece, like *Fidelio* or *Pelléas et Mélisande*. Stravinsky, uniquely, did both. *The Rake's Progress* is his only full-length opera, but it was preceded and followed by a variety of other works combining, as opera combines, music with words and gesture. It is as if he had been avoiding opera until the composition of *The Rake's Progress*, just as he had avoided the sonata until the Piano Sonata of 1924 and the symphony until the Symphony in C of 1938–40. And, exactly as in those other cases, the avoidance continues even in the eventual capitulation: *The Rake's Progress* is an opera despite itself.

Stravinsky's first operatic work was also his first project for the stage, *Solovey* or *The Nightingale*, to a Russian libretto by Stepan Mitusov after the tale by Hans Christian Andersen. He began work on it in 1908, shortly before the death of his teacher Rimsky-Korsakov, whose fantasy operas, along with Debussy, were a notable influence on the piece. But in 1909 he stopped work to compose his first ballet score for Dyagilev, *The Firebird*, and henceforth music for dancing was to occupy much of his attention. Only after writing *Petrushka* and *The Rite of Spring* did he return to *The Nightingale* and complete it in 1913–14, producing a work which, though having three acts, lasts for only about three-quarters of an hour in all. Thus was established the 'one-acter' size of Stravinsky's later quasi-operatic works, including *Oedipus rex* and *Perséphone*. Thus was established too the approach of opera towards ballet that was to dominate his thinking, since he subsequently described the two later acts of *The Nightingale* (those composed after *The Rite*) as 'a kind of opera–pageant ballet',[1] and the original production by Dyagilev's company placed the emphasis firmly on dance and spectacle. Stravinsky himself decided that the soprano who sings the Nightingale must be placed in the orchestra pit and represented on stage by the figure of a bird; Dyagilev also removed the singer who takes the part of the Fisherman and had this role mimed, following the precedent of his production of Rimsky's *The Golden Cockerel* in the same season, for which he had used a double cast of singers on either side of the stage and dancers executing the action.

The idea obviously appealed to Stravinsky. In a newspaper interview of 1913 he had maintained that: 'Music can be married to gesture or to words – not to both without bigamy.'[2] But his experience with *The Nightingale* had shown him how unions might be effected on separate planes, and this he pursued in his next works for the stage, *Svadebka* or *The Wedding* (1914–23) and *Bayka* or *Baize* (1915–16). Both are treatments of Russian folk material adapted by the composer himself. In both the action is danced while the singers, whose parts are not in any consistent direct relationship with the characters on stage, join the orchestra. And in both Stravinsky intended that the mismatch between music and drama should be manifest: he wanted the orchestras of singers and instrumentalists to be visible, to have their own visual identity, so undermining the illusion of opera that characters and music belong together in some imagined world.

The presentation of action and music as linked but distinct was taken further in *Histoire du soldat* (1918), where the play by Ramuz is managed by a narrator and enacted by two actors and a dancer, while an instrumental septet, also on stage, play a score which lies alongside and then comes to engulf the drama. His next ballet, *Pulcinella* (1919–20), again had singers in the pit for a few songs kept as relics of the 'Pergolesi' originals. Then, after this backward glance to Italian comic opera, Stravinsky turned to the operatic tradition of his own country and created in *Mavra* (1921–2) a short one-act opera in homage to Pushkin, Glinka and Tchaikovsky. They make a strange trinity. Glinka has commonly been seen as the ancestor of the Mighty Handful and their brand of Russian nationalism, but Stravinsky made it clear that he was thinking not of *Ruslan* but of the songs, and the way they adapt Italian bel canto to native substance, much as Pushkin and Tchaikovsky also looked westward. *Mavra* was a reaction against the Russianness of such works as *The Wedding*, which had celebrated their exoticism, and an assertion that the Russian artist must become heir to a wider heritage. It was the last work in which he set the Russian language, and the first in which he chose to revitalise old forms and styles.

But, characteristically, Stravinsky's neoclassicism in *Mavra* was not an acceptance of old conventions but a use of them to formalise and distance. If the speed and absurdity of the action were not enough to prevent its being taken as a slice of life, then the presence of arias and ensembles would show up the work as a construction, especially when these operatic routines are accompanied not by a balanced orchestra but by a wind band that belongs only to the period of composition. Thus although *Mavra* was the first work since *The Nightingale* in which Stravinsky had tried to bring about the bigamous union of music, language and movement, he still maintained a division between the bel canto voices and the jazzy accompaniment.

In his next two operatic works he reverted to making such a division between substance and form quite unmistakable. The opera–oratorio *Oedipus rex* (1926–7) was to be presented with a minimum of action by masked figures on pedestals, singing in Latin while a narrator introduces and explains the story in the vernacular, so that the myth is displayed rather than dramatised. Similarly in *Perséphone* (1933–4) Stravinsky wanted a gap between action and narrative, here with the story mimed and danced while it is also being told by a chorus, a tenor soloist and a female speaker.

The ritual aspect of *Oedipus rex* and *Perséphone* takes on a particular significance if one recalls that these were among the very few of Stravinsky's works since *Mavra* to employ voices, and that nearly all the others were religious: the *Symphony of Psalms* (1930), the cantata *Babel* (1944), the Mass (1944–8) and the small a cappella pieces. (The only exceptions were little homages to Ramuz and to Nadia Boulanger.) When he came to compose *The Rake's Progress*, therefore, he had for more than a quarter of a century kept to the principle that singing could be permitted only in the cases of a chorus expressing sacred truth or of participants retelling a quasi-sacred myth at a remove. Such a history could be a preparation only for an opera in inverted commas, an opera aware of itself at every moment as *Mavra* had been.

That any new opera would have to be also a number opera, like *Mavra*, *Oedipus rex* and *Perséphone*, is to be assumed from Stravinsky's spoken pronouncements, especially those in his *Poetics of Music* (1939–40). Although, as Robert Craft has demonstrated, the text of these lectures was in fact written by Roland-Manuel,[3] Stravinsky's notes make it clear that he was in sympathy with the belabouring of Wagner, writing that: 'Defiance (of the classical Rules) demands things of music that are beyond its jurisdiction -- the principle of illustration, imitation (leitmotiv).'[4] His draft also includes one statement central to the *Poetics*: 'Art is freer when it is more limited, more finished, canonical, dogmatic.'[5]

According to Stravinsky's own account, the possibility of *The Rake's*

Progress arose very much at the time of the *Poetics of Music*, since he had wanted to write an opera in English ever since his arrival in the United States, which was in 1939.[6] If so, it was a possibility that remained dormant for several years, since the pattern of his output during his early American years continued as it had been in France: the emphasis was on orchestral works, including the *Symphony in Three Movements* (1942–5), and ballet scores, ranging from the *Circus Polka* (1942) to *Orpheus* (1947). Then, while he was at work on *Orpheus*, he found the subject for his opera. On 2 May 1947 he visited a Hogarth exhibition at the Chicago Art Institute[7] and there saw the series of canvases entitled *The Rake's Progress*, painted in 1732–3 and normally housed in Sir John Soane's Museum in Lincoln's Inn Fields, London. Popular at the time in engravings, they depict a moral fable in eight stages:

1. 'The Heir': Tom Rakewell comes into his inheritance on the death of his father and is visited by Sarah Young, a town girl he has seduced, together with her mother.
2. 'The Levee': Tom is seen with various professors in the gentlemanly arts.
3. 'The Orgy': he rollicks with whores in a low tavern.
4. 'The Arrest': he is about to be apprehended for debt, but Sarah arrives with her savings to redeem him.
5. 'The Marriage': he makes a marriage of convenience to an elderly and ill-favoured rich lady, while Sarah, carrying his child in her arms, is excluded from the ceremony.
6. 'The Gaming House': he loses his second fortune.
7. 'The Prison': he is committed to the Fleet for debt.
8. 'The Madhouse': he is removed to an asylum, where the ever-faithful Sarah continues to visit him.

The paintings had been used as the basis for a ballet by the Vic-Wells company in 1935, with music by Gavin Gordon in a pastiche Handelian style and choreography by Ninette de Valois, and it would seem quite possible that Stravinsky knew of this. He may also have been aware of an updated film version, starring Rex Harrison, which had been made in 1945. In any event, he decided soon after seeing the pictures that within them lay the germ of a libretto, and so he set about finding a literary collaborator. If he had already decided on an opera in eighteenth-century dress, musical as well as scenic, then he might have been expected to look for an Italian poet, even if it is hard to think of anyone who could possibly have fulfilled his task. In fact he seems to have had no doubt that this would be his opera in English, and of course he had chosen an English subject; he therefore began by seeking the advice of his Californian friend and close neighbour Aldous Huxley.[8]

Huxley recommended W. H. Auden, whose claims might have been

2 Hogarth: 'The Orgy' from *The Rake's Progress* (1732–3)

supposed to rest not only on his volumes of poetry but also on his experience as a dramatist, with Christopher Isherwood in *The Ascent of F6* and other plays of the thirties, and, more particularly, on his creative association with Benjamin Britten on various stage, film and concert pieces.[9] Of all this work, however, Stravinsky knew only the commentary he had written for the Post Office film *Night Mail*,[10] with music by Britten, and he entrusted the first approach to his publisher Ralph Hawkes, who met Auden in New York on 30 September 1947,[11] only a week after the completion of *Orpheus*, and was able to report a favourable response.

Six days later Stravinsky wrote himself for the first time to Auden, outlining his project.[12] The most emphatic of his statements reiterates his anti-Wagnerianism: 'Bear in mind', he wrote, 'that I will compose *not* a Musical Drama, but just an Opera with definitely separated numbers connected by spoken (not sung) words of the text, because I want to avoid the customary operatic recitative.' And this is strange, because the eventual opera was in fact to contain recitative of the most exceedingly customary yet thoroughly Stravinskyan kind. One must suppose, then, that his first notions were of an opera quite different in kind from the work he went on to compose. If it had avoided recitative it would have done no more than follow the divergent precedents of *Mavra*, *Oedipus rex* and *Perséphone*, all of which had managed with none or very little, but a work consisting of arias, ensembles and choruses linked by spoken dialogue suggests something along the lines of the *opéras-comiques* that Roland-Manuel had had him praise in the *Poetics of Music*.[13] Such a hypothesis is strengthened by another remark in this first letter to Auden, that the two-act opera would include 'a Choreographic Divertissement in the first Act's finale' (in Stravinsky's vocabulary this does not imply anything especially whimsical or lighthearted: he had called *The Wedding* a divertissement). But if the initial idea was for an opera in the French mould, this was soon dropped, for on 9 November, before meeting Auden for close discussion, Stravinsky wrote to Hawkes asking for full scores of the Mozart–da Ponte operas and *Die Zauberflöte*, all to be the 'source of inspiration for my future opera'.[14]

It is also noteworthy that his first letter to his librettist should have included among its few details the idea that the opera should end with the hero 'in an asylum scratching a fiddle'. This would have come from Hogarth's final painting, where the fiddle player is one of Tom's mad fellow inmates, but, seen in the light of *Histoire du soldat*, where the violin is a central prop and musical presence as the image of the Soldier's

3 Hogarth: 'The Madhouse' from *The Rake's Progress* (1732–3)

soul, the suggestion may imply that the Hogarthian morality was already being overlaid in Stravinsky's mind by a Faust narrative. It was not spoken of again, except by Auden in his reply asking 'do you want the fiddle to run through the story?', and dropped back to its original significance, for the stage direction to the last scene asks for 'a blind man with a broken fiddle' among the chorus of madmen. But its implications, if implications they were, became central.

At this early stage in his dealings with Auden, however, Stravinsky was anxious as much to convey the style he wanted as to delimit the opera's content. The text would have to take note of Hogarth's period, his letter continued, but it ought to be 'as contemporary as I treated Pergolesi in my PULCINELLA'. And in thus calling for a baroque subject worked in modern diction he was assuring himself a willing reply from the poet.

Auden's experience of operatic writing, when he received Stravinsky's invitation in October 1947, was considerably less wide and various than the composer's. In his work on plays and films he had had to create texts of diverse kinds to be set by Britten, but his only script for the musical stage so far was the libretto of the 'choral operetta' he had written with Britten in New York, *Paul Bunyan* (1941). However, in the intervening years his interest in opera had been stimulated by his friend Chester Kallman: in 1948, when he was asked to give a list of favourite recordings, he was to limit himself almost exclusively to opera, this personal repertory including Mozart, Bellini, Donizetti, Weber, Verdi and Wagner.[15]

He wrote back enthusiastically in answer to Stravinsky's letter,[16] and made some suggestions of his own, including that of a 'choric parabasis' between the acts, though in the event such a direct speech from the stage was to be made under more Mozartian cover in the form of an Epilogue. Stravinsky and his new-found librettist then spent a week together at the composer's house, from 11 to 18 November 1947, during which time they attended a local performance of an opera that was to have a great effect on their own, *Così fan tutte*. However, the composer can hardly have been impressed by the scoring on this particular occasion, since the orchestra was replaced by a pair of pianos.[17]

The two men also prepared while together a draft scenario[18] which is remarkably close to the final opera in its narrative outline, with the principal exception that the Auction scene was to conclude Act II instead of starting Act III: the work had already grown from two acts to three, although a few months after the première Stravinsky was to change his mind and declare his preference for a single interval after Baba's and Tom's homecoming.[19] The 1947 scenario is even close to the eventual work in the placing and nature of musical numbers. And now the recitative principle has been introduced, though with a proposed piano accompaniment: indeed, Stravinsky feared problems of balance if a harpsichord were used and did not decide to authorise it, with the piano remaining as alternative, until the work was finished.[20]

Since the draft scenario was put together during a time when Stravinsky and Auden were working together, it is impossible to determine just what was contributed by each. What is certainly clear, however, is that the plot was suddenly developed far beyond Hogarth. Where the original Tom Rakewell was simply a wastrel who got his just deserts, the hero of the scenario is an intellectual weakling who falls prey to the cynical arguments of the unnamed 'Villain' — a character quite absent from the paintings. Hero and villain become in the first scene, as they do in the final opera, master and servant, a coupling which Auden once described as peculiarly suitable to the artistic expression of 'the inner dialogue of human personality'.[21] They are thus to be seen as aspects of one individual — embodiments, in Auden's terms, of Ego and self — and so when the villain gains a name it is Shadow (his other name, Nick, has of course quite other connotations). One consequence of introducing the villain to bring Tom news of his inheritance, as Auden soon realised, was that his wealth had to be unexpected, and so he was made the heir not of his father, as he still is in the draft, but of an obscure uncle.[22]

The draft also transmutes the townee Sarah Young into a country girl, eventually given the name Anne Trulove, a change which assists the mechanics of the plot and also brings into the opera a fruitful contrast between the natural life of the country and the rule of artifice in the metropolis. The other woman in Tom's life is the 'Ugly Duchess', whom he marries in response to the villain's instruction concerning the nature of marriage: she has yet to become the grotesque of the opera, Baba the Turk, chosen by Tom at Shadow's prompting to demonstrate the freedom of his will to ignore inclination and convention. Already, however, the scenario has the double-focus classicism of the final opera, situating the action in the eighteenth century while alluding through it to the myth of Venus and Adonis. There were ample precedents for this in Stravinsky's output, especially in the ballets *Apollo, Perséphone* and *Orpheus*, but in all these cases the reference to the eighteenth and seventeenth centuries was entirely a matter of musical style, not of setting. *The Rake's Progress*, in draft and in its finished form, made a departure in bringing this irony on to the stage, with characters who know themselves to be created on the pattern of classical figures.

Stravinsky found in Auden an admirable and sympathetic collaborator, as his tribute to him testifies,[23] and he was particularly impressed by the poet's passion for technique and his relish of art as a strictly regulated game.[24] After their week together he was able to report to Hawkes that all had gone well, mentioning that he expected to be writing for 'an orchestra of about 35',[25] and indeed the scoring was to be of chamber proportions, with double wind, no trombones and no percussion apart from the sparingly used timpani. In December 1947 he began the music, composing first the string quartet prelude to the Graveyard scene,[26] even though he had not yet received any of the libretto.

That was being written at the same time by Auden with, as yet unknown to Stravinsky, the assistance of Kallman: the composer was told of this only when the first act of the text was delivered to him in January 1948,[27] the remainder following within the next month.[28] Though Stravinsky was somewhat discomfited by the dual authorship when he had been expecting to receive Auden's unaided work, he was in no position to object to what was a *fait accompli*. He therefore graciously accepted a libretto for which the authorial responsibilities were, according to a letter from Auden to Robert Craft,[29] as follows:

Act I scene 1: W.H.A. to the end of the aria 'Since it is not by merit', then C.K.
Act I scene 2: C.K.
Act I scene 3: W.H.A.
Act II scene 1: C.K. to the end of the aria reprise 'Always the quarry', then W.H.A.
Act II scene 2: C.K.
Act II scene 3: W.H.A.
Act III scene 1: C.K., with off-stage words for Tom and Shadow by W.H.A.
Act III scene 2: C.K.
Act III scene 3: W.H.A.
Epilogue: W.H.A.

It is extremely doubtful, however, whether anyone would be able to detect the two voices without being told which was which, and in any case the authorship is partly confused by revisions to the libretto, about which more is said in the note by Robert Craft which follows in Chapter 3 below. For example, in versifying Baba's part in the trio of Act II scene 2 Auden was making a change to Kallman's text.

Any ill feeling between the composer and his librettists over the joint authorship evaporated when Stravinsky met Kallman on 5 April 1948 and was charmed.[30] Then on 8 May he began the composition of the opera in earnest, beginning now at the beginning of the text.[31] On

2 August he wrote to Hawkes to say that he had not quite finished the first scene, because although the opera was affording him 'great joy and freshness' and would be 'very easy to listen to', there was the problem that 'making this easiness is very expensive with my time'.[32] Even so, he completed the first act on 16 January 1949 and played it over to Auden on 3 February, on which occasion the librettist suggested that Anne's aria at the end of the act ought to be made to end on a high C, and wrote a new line on the spot to make this possible.[33]

Auden's readiness to make changes to suit the music was in line with the modest principle put forward in an essay he published to coincide with the première of the opera:[34]

the verses which the librettist writes are not addressed to the public but are really a private letter to the composer. They have their moment of glory, the moment in which they suggest to him a certain melody; once that is over they are as expendable as infantry to a Chinese general: they must efface themselves and cease to care what happens to them.

It would be quite unfair to Auden and Kallman to judge their work as poetry, therefore, but at the same time it is impossible not to notice the great skill with which they fulfilled their task. Again Auden's essay, though written after the event, gives the clue to the libretto's virtues. He mentions that the 'drama of recognition must be tropically abrupt', as indeed it is in the Graveyard scene, because 'song cannot walk, it can only jump'. He observes too that 'the librettist need never bother his head, as the dramatist must, about probability', and certainly he and Kallman do not seem to have been greatly inhibited by what is plausible. But they have their justification, because, as Auden goes on to state: 'No good opera plot can be sensible for people do not sing when they are feeling sensible.'

Sudden turns and unlikely chances were thus deliberately placed to stimulate the composer, an end served also by the variety of verse forms provided by the libretto. In general the text offers the pretext for arias, ensembles and choruses in verse linked by prose passages for recitative or arioso: the principal exception is Shadow's 'Fair lady, gracious gentlemen' in the first scene, which is written in prose but composed as an aria (though called 'Recitative' in the score). 'The crowning glory of opera', Auden wrote in his essay, 'is the big ensemble', and he created opportunities for numbers of this kind in the quartet of Act I scene 1, the trio of Act II scene 2 and the stretto—finale of Act III scene 1: in each case the simultaneous expression of different feelings is helped by cunning connections of metre and rhyme among the voices.

Within solo numbers the poetic technique is similarly adroit in proposing various kinds of musical treatment. In Act II scene 1, for example, Tom's opening aria is written in iambic tetrameters with a break in the middle of the line, inviting the composer to set them in a slow 4/8 rhythm:

> Vary the song, O London, change!
> Disband your notes and let them range,
> Let rumour scream, let folly purr,
> Let tone desert the flatterer.

By contrast, the verse movement of Shadow's aria later in the same scene is much quicker, and the ballad couplets lend themselves to a fast 3/8 musical setting:

> In youth the panting slave pursues
>   The fair evasive dame;
> Then, caught in colder fetters, woos
>   Wealth, office or a name;

It is also surely not by accident that the most classical of English lines, the iambic pentameter, is reserved for the opening duet in which Tom and Anne sing of spring idyll and a Golden Age.

So apt was the libretto to operatic setting, and so amicable was the collaboration, that all three authors seem to have imagined their creative relationship would soon continue to other works. In 1949 Auden mooted the idea of 'a comic libretto about the Muse and her relations with Berlioz, Mendelssohn and Rossini',[35] for which the draft interestingly insists on orchestrally accompanied recitative rather than the secco of *The Rake's Progress*.[36] Nothing came of this, but Auden and Kallman did produce in 1952 the complete text for a piece in one act, *Delia, or A Masque of Night*,[37] which Stravinsky announced to his publishers he would set,[38] but in the event did not because he found he 'could not continue in the same strain'.[39] He did choose from Auden's anthology of English verse for the words of his Cantata (1951–2), but that work is already distant from *The Rake's Progress* in style, and when in 1953 he began preparations for a new opera it was in collaboration with Dylan Thomas, whose death in that year cut the project short – and prompted the dirge-canons and song *In memoriam Dylan Thomas* (1954) which confirmed the serial direction of Stravinsky's thinking.

Auden and Kallman remained his friends, and in 1964 Auden provided the text for his *Elegy for J.F.K.* for baritone and three clarinets. But during this last phase of his creative career there were to be only two more dramatic works, the ballet *Agon* (1953–7) and the television piece *The Flood* (1961–2), for which Robert Craft assembled words from Genesis and from English mystery plays, and in which Stravinsky returned to the amalgamation of different means he had essayed in *Histoire du soldat*, this time using dance, song, speech over music and choral set-pieces. The librettists, however, continued to indulge the taste for operatic writing they had discovered in *The Rake's Progress*, so that Stravinsky's opera had its various progeny in Henze's *Elegy for Young Lovers* (1959–61), *The Bassarids* (1965) and *Moralities* (1969, by Auden alone), in Chávez's *The Visitors* (1953–6, by Kallman alone), in Nicholas Nabokov's *Love's Labour's Lost* (1973) and in translations of works by Mozart, Dittersdorf and Weill.[40]

3 A note on the sketches and the two versions of the libretto
BY ROBERT CRAFT

Perhaps the most striking feature of the sketches is that, while they differ on every page from the final score, almost all of the first notations for a piece or passage are remarkably similar to the ultimate versions. In only one significant instance did Stravinsky alter his original choice of metre, transforming the march rhythm

| 2/4 Lanter - loo | my la - dy |

into the 6/8 dance. Changes of key, or tonality, after the first draft, are almost as infrequent. The principal exceptions are: 'O heart be stronger', of which Stravinsky composed a few bars in C minor before lowering it to B minor, 'Venus, mount thy throne' (see Plate 9 in the facsimile sketches below) and the second choral response in the lullaby of Act III scene 3, which was originally in the same key as the first response until Stravinsky discovered the effect of the upward transposition.

Changes in melodic intervals between sketches and final score are numerous but rarely crucial. One important exception is found between the first and final drafts of the music in which Shadow enumerates the means by which Rakewell might choose to die. In the original, the melodic line is confined to seconds; the wide intervals were developed later. Words are sometimes found in purely rhythmic form, without pitches or harmonic 'blocking', though these rhythms are often changed from one draft to another. In the sketch of the Act III lullaby, for example, the dotted rhythm in the first measure is continued, while at '[Be thou] insane', the figure ♩♩ occurs on every beat of the bar, including the first; Stravinsky introduced the rests, like the note itself, Shadow's E natural, after second or subsequent thoughts.

Indications for instrumentation are found throughout the sketches, but not many of them differ significantly from the final score. A trombone makes an appearance in the accompaniment at 'The Age of Gold'; horns, rather than trumpets, are indicated at fig. 33 in Act II; and at

Baba's 'My love, am I to remain in here forever?' Stravinsky's first preference was for cor anglais and bassoon instead of two bassoons.

A comparison of the sketches and final score reveals many improvements in pacing. To mention only one, Rakewell's acceptance of Shadow's pact — 'A fair offer, 'tis agreed' — was originally followed by a perfect cadence, and by some notations for a new piece in F, in 3/16 time. The next draft contains the elision to A minor.

Virtually no music was discarded, apart from *ossia* versions of brief phrases. The one exception is found at fig. 46 in Act III scene 1. Here Stravinsky wrote, and promptly cancelled, a two-bar interlude for flute and clarinet — which could be restored, since a break in Sellem's part at this point would afford relief.

Finally, it should be said that on first reading the libretto Stravinsky was exasperated by Shadow's philosophical asides in the Graveyard scene — 'The positive appals him', and 'the simpler the trick'. By the time Stravinsky reached this point in the composition, however, he treasured every word of the libretto and cut or changed very few of them.

Stravinsky wrote the 'summary sketch score' in pencil on large sheets of Manila, drawing all of the staves with his stylus. In comparatively dense passages, such as the quartet in Act I scene 1, he used blue and red pencil to clarify the part-writing. Many separate sketch pages of different sizes are clipped to the Manila ones or folded within them. Only eighteen entries in the summary sketch score are dated:

11 December 1947	Completes the prelude to Act III scene 2 in sketch and in full score.

Act I

8 May 1948	Begins the opera at fig. 2. (The prelude, not dated, was written after the Epilogue, in April 1951.)
17 July 1948	Completes the music through 'You are a rich man.'
13 September 1948	Completes the duettino.
3 October 1948	Completes scene 1 (except that the repeat in the terzettino was added at a later date).
5 October 1948	Begins scene 2.
16 January 1949	Completes Act I.
28 July 1949	Completes Act I in full score (though the dates of the completion of each act in the full score are misleading, since Stravinsky orchestrated as he composed).

Act II

1 April 1949	Begins Act II with 'Vary the song.'
29 August 1949	'O heart be stronger.'

End October 1949	Begins trio ('Could it then?').
3 November 1949	Completes trio.
18 December 1949	Begins Baba's 'As I was saying'.
29 December 1949	Completes Baba's D minor aria.
10 January 1950	'Oh Nick, I've had the strangest dream.'
1 February 1950	Completes Act II in full score.

Act III

End May 1950	Begins 'What curious phenomena?'
29 October 1950	Completes scene 2.
28 January 1951	Completes the opera to 'Madmen, where have you hidden her?'
7 April 1949	Completes the Epilogue in orchestra score, as well as Act III.

On 5 June 1951 Stravinsky composed the definitive version of the two bars before fig. 51 in Act I. On 10 July he added bars 6–7 of fig. 197 in Act III; Auden had written the words, 'To crop the Spring's return', in the Lombardy Hotel, New York, at the beginning of April 1950, on a sheet of hotel stationery that Stravinsky evidently misplaced.

The following excerpts from the sketches require little comment.[1] Plate 4 (from the beginning of Act I scene 1) reveals that Stravinsky began not with the woodwind introduction but with the first sentence of the libretto (whose setting here does not resolve the arguments about harmonic and accentual ambiguities, especially since the minim in the bass is positioned under the second beat in a 3/4 bar!). Plate 5 (from Shadow's monologue in Act I scene 1) provides an instance of a sketch remote in key, contour, instrumentation and metre from the final version. Plate 6 shows Stravinsky improving on his first setting of the words from Anne's aria in Act I scene 3 'Although I weep'. In Plate 7 he can be seen giving thought and weight to the setting of Rakewell's accompanied recitative in Act II scene 1, 'Who's honest, chaste, or kind?' – and placing the solution in abeyance while composing the music for Rakewell's answer, 'One, only one'. In Plate 8, Stravinsky's momentum at the conclusion of a piece is seen carrying him through the next words, 'Or I die' (from Tom's dialogue with the Madmen in Act III scene 3); then, no doubt pausing to give them due importance, he wrote the final version in the next entry. In Plate 9 A major is seen to have been the first choice of key for Tom's arioso in Act III scene 3, 'Venus, mount thy throne.'

The transcription of the 'First Scenario' published in *Memories and Commentaries* is inaccurate and incomplete. The page (no. 6) containing the trio with chorus at the end of Act III scene 1 is missing, probably because this scene was not drafted during the sessions in Stravinsky's

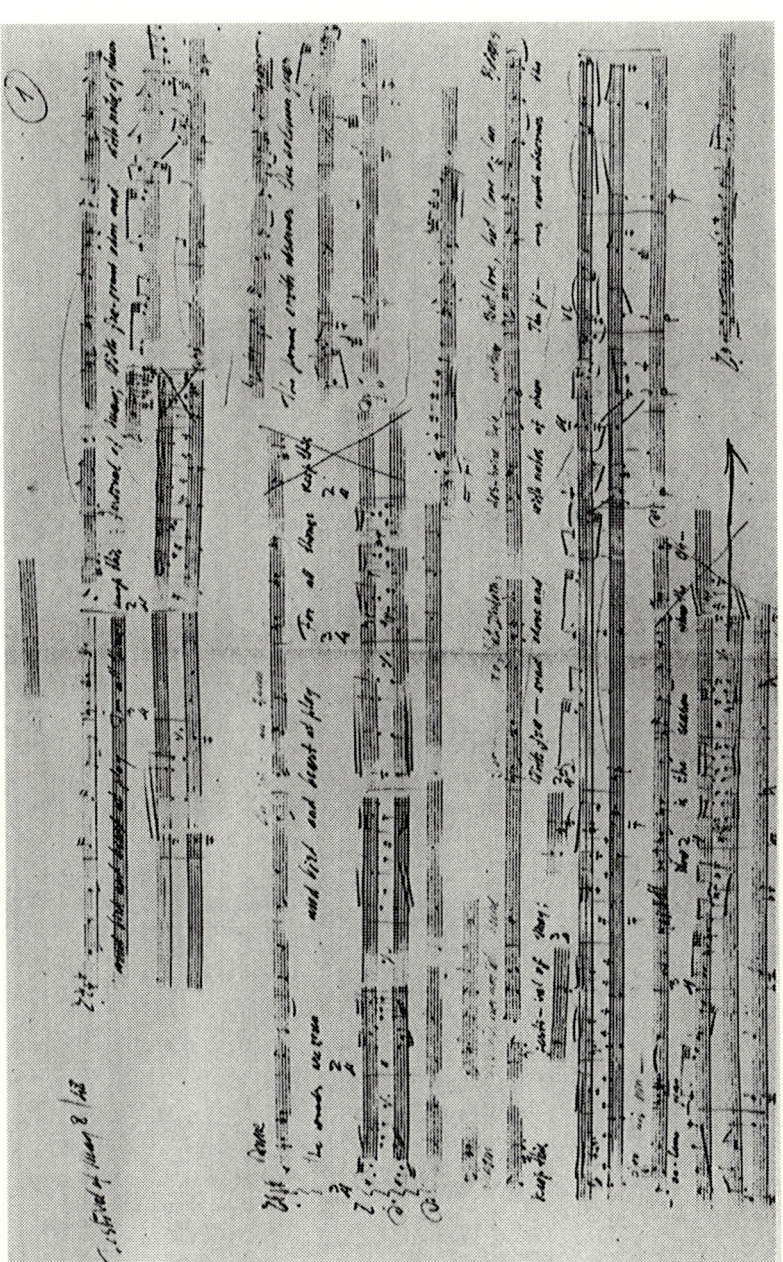

4 Sketch of the beginning of Act I scene 1

5 Sketch from Shadow's monologue in Act I scene 1

6 Sketch from Anne's aria in Act I scene 3

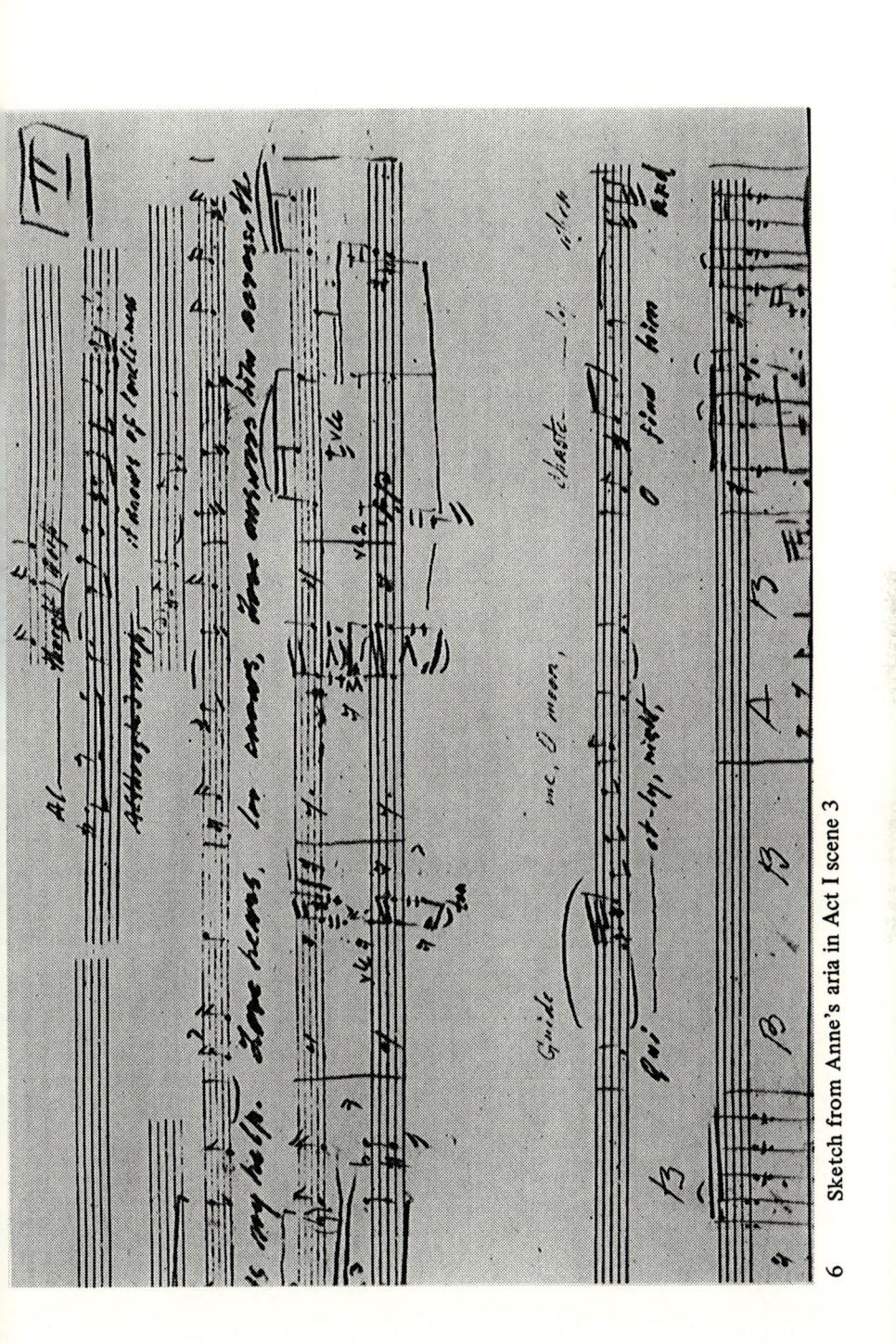

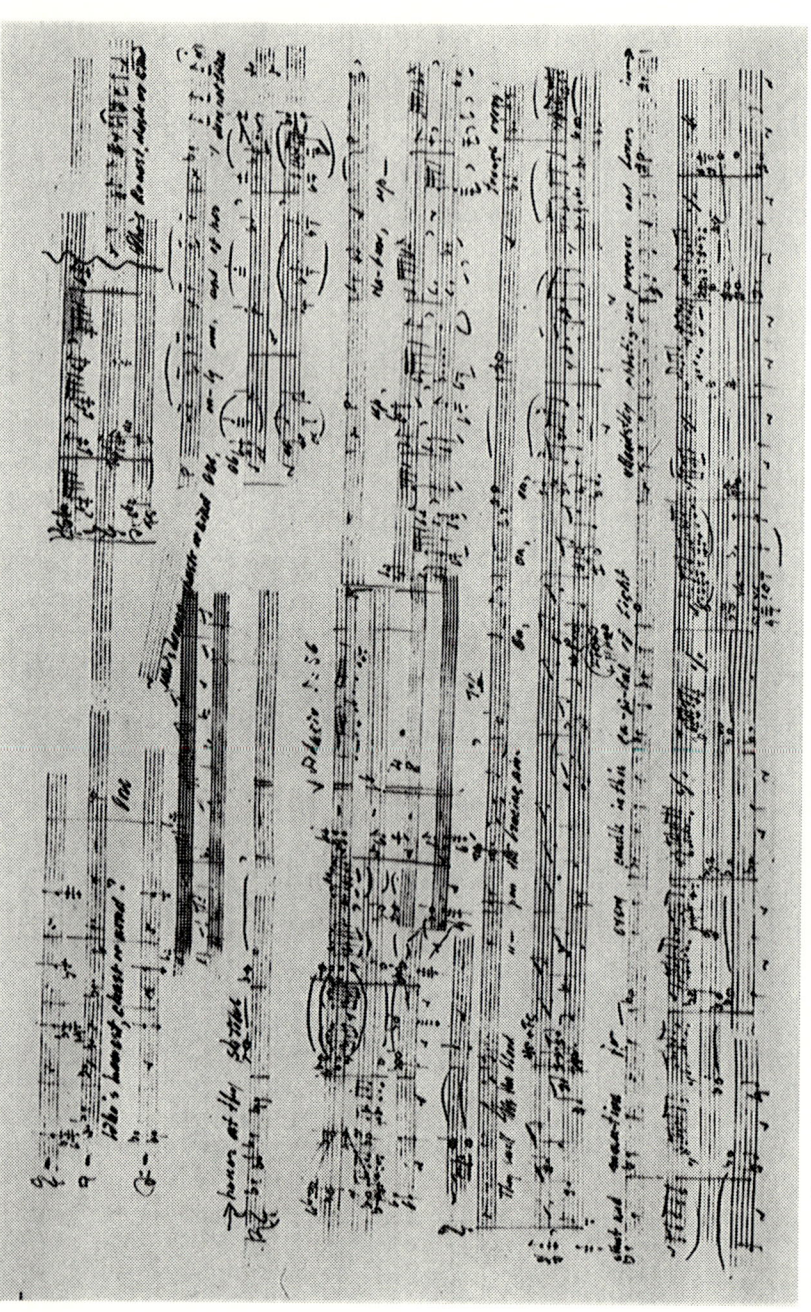

7 Sketch from Tom's accompanied recitative in Act II scene 1

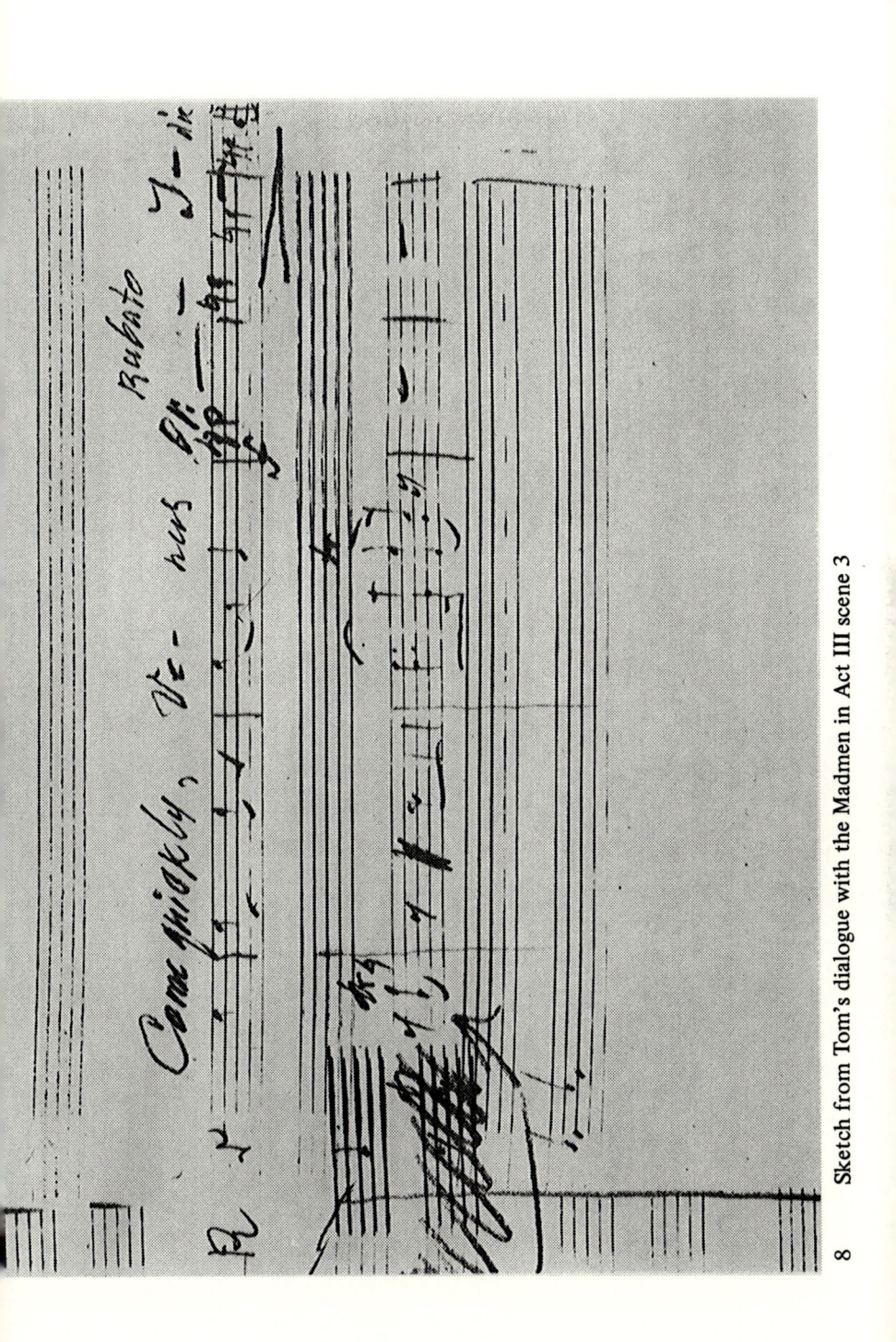

8 Sketch from Tom's dialogue with the Madmen in Act III scene 3

9 Sketch from Tom's arioso in Act III scene 3

home and because the page is in the hand of Kallman, for which reason Stravinsky did not file it under 'Auden'. Kallman also contributed a 'Note on the suggested two-part structure' of this scene. (Part I begins with Anne's 'He loves me still', part II with Baba's 'I shall go back'.) Stravinsky followed the suggestion but added an introduction (Baba: 'You love him') and an interlude (Baba: 'So find him').

Some of Stravinsky's and Auden's handwritten corrections and additions are missing from the five pages of the scenario that were published, including the composer's notation at the end, 'Hollywood, Nov. 18/1947', and the poet's repeated instruction for Shadow to whistle (rather than to laugh) at each exit and entrance. But obviously the complete scenario must be made available before a satisfactory study of the dramatic conception of the opera can be undertaken. It is in the scenario, after all, that directors have found justification for dividing Acts II and III into four and two scenes respectively.

Stravinsky received the libretto in three instalments, in January and February 1948; the pact between Shadow and Rakewell, not found in the original (!), where the text goes directly from Shadow's 'All is ready, sir' to Rakewell's 'Dear father Trulove', was sent separately on 9 February. On 31 March, in Washington, DC, Auden presented the composer with a substantially revised version of the whole. By this date, however, Stravinsky had added so many marginal notes and scansion and other marks, that the first version was the one from which he composed the opera, in spite of the many changes and inserts that this required. But more surprising than any of the changes that he introduced is his retention of Auden's favourite heading, 'Orchestral Recitative'. Stravinsky kept this even when it did not fit the music. Thus Shadow's 'Fair lady' aria is called 'Recitative and Quartet' in the published score, even though the recitative comes only at the end of the piece, and 'Quartet' is the title of the next one.

Stravinsky's queries in his working copy of the libretto were numerous, but he erased nearly all of them. The few that remain are characteristically waspish. After Auden's note, 'Return of the orchestra', Stravinsky wrote: 'It never stopped.' And following the stage direction for Baba, 'Brushes herself off while the chorus murmurs . . .', Stravinsky pencilled the objection: *'During* her aria or *after it,* not *while . . .'* At one place in Act III, the composer inserted the question: 'What is the difference, for the music, between "chorus" and "crowd"?'

Most of Stravinsky's comments in the 'Washington' libretto are in Russian, probably for the reason that, with Auden watching, the composer was afraid of making mistakes in English. At the end of the Brothel scene, however, Stravinsky *did* write in English, though at a later date: 'What are doing the men and women during Shadow's last lines?' (No stage direction is given after the chorus forms 'a lane' for Mother Goose and Rakewell.)

In the revised version of the cabaletta, the line 'Or freed unwanted' had become 'Or be rejected', but during the meeting in Washington this was further amended to 'Or be forgotten'. And whereas, in the original, the preceding recitative ends with the words 'Tom is weak', the revision adds: 'And wants the comfort of a helping hand' (abruptly changed to 'And needs the comfort of a faithful hand'). In Washington, or soon after, the line 'This engine shall all men excite' was changed to the less risqué 'This engine Adam shall excite.' On that 31 March, too, Auden added prosodic markings for the alternating 8- and 6-syllable verse beginning 'In youth the panting slave pursues'; decided that the 'tea cosy' of the first version and 'dust cover' of the second should become 'the wig'; and, in response to Stravinsky's criticism of wordiness, Auden wrote 'Omit if too much', and 'could be cut' next to several passages, including the quatrain 'Defeated, mocked' and the two choral stanzas, 'In triumph glorious' and 'For what is sweeter?' But Stravinsky set every word, after resolving his doubts about some of them ('o'er', to name only one).

The next major revision, made at Stravinsky's request in October 1949 and sent to him by Auden on the 24th, was Baba's part in the terzettino. Her lines in both the original and revised versions had been the same:

I *believe* I explained that I was waiting . . . *Who* can this person be? . . . It could hardly be thought that wedded bliss entailed *such* manner of attention . . . I confess that I do *not* understand . . . When am I to be helped from this infernal box? . . . Should I expire, the world will know whom to blame . . . Tell her to go, you have your duties as a spouse, you know, and I cannot but feel this is the least of them . . . Allah! . . . I'm suffocating . . . Hussy, begone, or I shall summon spirits and have you well haunted for your presumption . . . A plague upon matrimony . . . My love, if you do not wish Baba to be piqued, do see that she is not condemned to remain immured in this conveyance forever.

Auden now changed this to the following, marking the stresses as well, and dividing the text into metrical units:

| Why this de- | lay? A- | way, [or the | crowd will] | O!
[And | why, if I | may be al- | lowed to in- | quire, does my
| husband de- | sire

Note on the sketches and two versions of libretto 29

Tŏ cŏn- | verse wīth thīs | persŏn?] | Whō īs īt, | prāy,
Hē prĕ- | fērs tō hīs | Bābă ŏn thēir | wēddīng | dāy?

Ă | fămĭlў | frīend? Ăn | ānciĕnt | flāme?
[Ă | brīde hăs | surelў thĕ | priŏr | clāim
Ŏn thē | brīdăl | nīght!] I'm | quīte pĕr- | plēxed
Ănd | mōre, Ĭ cŏn- | fĕss, thăn ă | trīfle | vēxed.

Ĕ- | nōugh īs ĕ- | nōugh! | Bābă īs nŏt | ūsed
Tŏ bē | sō ă- | būsed. Shē īs | nŏt ă- | mūsed.
Cŏme | hēre mў | lōve. Ĭ | hāte | wāiting.
I'm | sūffŏ- | cāting. | Hēavĕns ă- | bōve!
| Wīll yŏu pĕr- | mīt mĕ tō | sīt īn thīs cŏn- | vēyănce
Fŏr | ĕvĕr ănd | ĕvĕr?

Stravinsky did not set the words indicated above in brackets, and, of course, the accents and longs and shorts in the music of the third stanza are much more free and fluent than in the rhythmic scheme shown here.

Other changes were made in New York in April 1950. To give only two examples, 'I wish for nothing else' replaced 'Wishful chance, farewell', and 'such a hectic' day was substituted for 'such a thrilling' one. But by this time, why did Auden *not* cut

> Attorneys crouched like gardeners to pay,
> Bowers of paper only seals repair

which, whatever the lines mean, could make the audience wonder about the relevance of amphibious mammals? Auden had difficulties with Sellem's lines beginning 'An unknown object draws us near', and he temporarily deleted one of them, 'A block of copal? Mint of alchemy?', in order to insert the following line before the last one: 'O you whose houses are in order, hear.' The Washington text, however, introduces two lines after the first one ('An unknown object draws us, draws us near') that are even worse:

> They cannot face the future who have fear;
> Who does, beyond the Almanack shall peer.

In the first version of the libretto, Shadow uses 'thee' and 'thy' when addressing Rakewell in the Graveyard scene, but in one of the New York meetings Stravinsky insisted on 'you' and 'yours'. At first, too, the 'Fugal Chorus (Funèbre)', as Auden called it, consisted of the two lines:

> Mourn for Adonis, ever young, the dear
> Of Venus: weep, tread softly round his bier.

He expanded these later to four stanzas, consisting of lines of five, six, seven and eight syllables, respectively. Since, apart from a few canons and a brief chaconne, the opera does not employ contrapuntal forms, Stravinsky confined the 'fugal' idea to simple three-part imitations at the beginning of the chorus. Regrettably, he chose the octosyllabic lines, with the unfortunate silent possessive ('Venus'') – for which he added a syllable ('Venus's') and more music.

It should also be mentioned that on 7 August 1958, BBC television transmitted a performance of the 'second part' of the opera, with a prologue in rhymed couplets by Auden (and possibly Kallman), a synopsis of the first part, to be read by Nick Shadow. The televised portion of the opera apparently began with Act II scene 3, since the camera is directed to 'pull back' from Shadow at his lines

> So to our play. The wedding-knot is tied,
> And now you'll meet the bridegroom and the bride.

As the librettists' afterview interpretation of their drama, the text, of approximately sixty lines, sheds light on several questions, among them Rakewell's decision to marry Baba. Shadow says to him

> Be happy and rejoice,
> Knowing you know no motive for your choice

and explains to the audience that

> pride
> Soon won his guilty conscience to my side.

4 Synopsis

The generic naming of the opera's numbers here follows the score, with a few editorial additions in square brackets.

Prelude

Before the curtain rises there is a brisk, buoyant, fanfare-like summons scored essentially for the trumpets and horns. The key is E major, dominant of the A major which is prominent in the first and last scenes.

Act I

Scene 1

The garden of Trulove's house in the country during a spring afternoon. His daughter Anne and her beloved Tom Rakewell are seated in an arbour downstage.
Duet and trio. 'The woods are green.' The atmosphere of a pastoral idyll is conjured at once by the introduction, scored for a quartet of reed instruments: oboe, cor anglais and two bassoons. This introduction also establishes the key of A major, in which Anne begins the duet, singing of springtime and happiness coming with the 'festival of May'. Tom then enters, in G major, with a stanza which imitates Anne's and draws on a classical reference which will, during the course of the opera, become more than a conceit: Venus, the 'Cyprian Queen', brings love to make time revert, restore 'the Age of Gold'. Also restored, by the end of his solo, is the key of A major, in which he and Anne sing of their love, but there is a movement towards B major at the entrance of Trulove. While they sing on he adds a warning aside, hoping that all may be as it seems but knowing that no-one can be sure of another's heart or even of his own. The number ends with a further duet passage in A major and a little postlude for oboe, cor anglais and bassoon, re-

calling the introduction. There will be a similar A—B—A pattern to many of the arias and ensembles that follow.

Recitative [secco]. 'Anne, my dear'. Trulove comes forward and sends his daughter off to the kitchen. When she has gone he tells Tom the good news that he has secured him a position in a countinghouse in the city. Tom is less than delighted, remarking that he has other ideas, and Trulove is displeased. Tom airily assures him that his daughter will not have a poor husband, but Trulove's concern is rather that his son-in-law be not dishonest or lazy. He leaves abruptly, presumably not hearing Tom's opinion of him: 'The old fool!'

Recitative. 'Here I stand', with orchestra. In proud C major, with an emphasis on G as dominant, Tom declares that he will never accept the role of apprentice or drudge. Philosophers have determined that good works are of no account because everything is predestined (B major – E major), and so he will entrust himself to Fortune (concluding in F major).

Aria. 'Since it is not by merit'. Tom develops his theme – literally, since the music of his aria is infested by the motif to which he had sung the word 'Fortune': a scale fragment made up of a pair of semiquavers followed by a longer note. There are five short stanzas in an A—A—B—A—A pattern, the first accompanied only by two bassoons of which one is in canon with the voice at the octave – an example of several simple canons in the opera. Since the benefits of life are determined by fate rather than merit, Tom argues, there is no point in doing anything to help oneself: he will trust to his luck and his wishes. The key of the aria is F major, whose hunting-horn associations are underlined by the jaunty 2/4 rhythm and the little postlude. After this Tom says: 'I wish I had money', the first of his four spoken wishes.

Recitative [secco]. 'Tom Rakewell?'. In answer to Tom's wish, Shadow appears immediately at the garden gate, introduced by a harpsichord flourish. Tom is taken by surprise, but an imitating flourish, played quietly by a bassoon, suggests that he is on the point of recognising Shadow as his *alter ego*. However, the newcomer takes charge of the proceedings, and they make their introductions in F sharp. Shadow then promises Tom a 'bright future' on a high E all the more sinister for coming in an ambience of E flat. He mentions an uncle, of whom Tom has never heard, and then asks Tom to call his friends to hear some good news.

Recitative. 'Fair lady, gracious gentlemen'. Though so called in the score, this is really an aria for Shadow, followed by a short passage of recitative. The key is G major, in which Shadow tells of the uncle,

Synopsis

whom he served, and who made money abroad. But his fortune was of no use to him when he lay dying (A major), homesick and lovelorn (B minor, solos for flute and bassoon). And so – here Shadow returns to G major and to the manner of his opening – the uncle left his money to Tom, with whom, in his choice of key, Shadow has affirmed his identity.

Quartet. 'I wished but once.' This elaborate number begins with Tom reflecting, in B flat major and accompanied by a cello solo, on how his wish has come true as he was sure it would. He thanks Shadow, who in turn thanks him, for without a master, he remarks, he would soon die. Anne and her father then join the ensemble, giving their thanks to God: she prays that she will soon be married, he that Tom's pride will be curbed and that Anne will not be unhappy. With a change of key, to F major, and of metre, from 6/8 to 2/4, Tom and Anne reaffirm their love and Trulove calls down God's blessing on them. But Shadow interposes to turn the music towards F minor for a final modulatory section. Tom, he says, must come with him to see to his affairs. Tom replies that business can wait, but Trulove lends his weight to Shadow's advice. So Tom resolves to go, and in his final solo the music reinforces his determination with a firm return to B flat major.

Recitative [secco]. 'I'll call the coachman, sir.' After a short exchange Shadow and Trulove leave to make the travelling arrangements.

Duettino. 'Farewell, farewell'. With the reed instruments again to the fore – there is a gentle introduction for oboes, clarinets and bassoon – and now in Tom's and Shadow's G major, Anne and Tom bid each other adieu and promise undying love.

Recitative [secco]. 'All is ready, sir.' Trulove and Shadow return, and the servant tells his new master that all is ready for them to go. Tom asks what wages Shadow would deem appropriate, but Shadow, joined by the bassoons in the unsettling key of B flat minor, says that they will settle their account a year and a day hence, when Tom will have to pay only what he himself regards as just. Tom is evidently unworried either by the strangeness of the offer or by the associations of the term proposed, and he readily agrees.

Arioso. 'Dear father Trulove'. In A minor, accompanied only by the strings, Tom promises to send for Anne and her father as soon as his affairs are in order, and declares that then London will be at her feet. There is a tranquil orchestral transition, scored for clarinets, bassoons, horns, violins and violas, during which all take their leave of each other. Anne is moved, but Tom does not notice this.

Terzettino. 'Laughter and light'. There is a return to A major for this final number of the scene, in which Tom, Anne and Trulove separately reflect on the turn of events. Tom is confident that the world lies open to him on whom Fortune smiles; Anne sees Tom's happiness and wonders why she cannot share it wholeheartedly; Trulove fears that easy gain may only encourage Tom's sins. Finally they say their farewells. Shadow holds open the garden gate and then, as the tonality moves suddenly from A major to G major, he turns to the audience with the words 'The Progress of a Rake begins.' Thus Tom's key, seemingly innocent in the opening duet and the duettino, becomes in the last three bars of the scene ominous, opening the gate to his downfall.

Scene 2

Mother Goose's brothel in London. Tom, Shadow and Mother Goose are drinking together, surrounded by whores and roaring boys.
[**Introduction and chorus**]. 'With air commanding and weapon handy'. The full orchestra, so far used only at the end of Tom's aria 'Since it is not by merit', plays a boisterous introduction in C major, with a tipsy middle section in B major. This leads into a chorus in five stanzas, A–B–A–B–A, the first and third for the men (roaring boys) in C major but resting on the dominant, the second and fourth for the women (whores) in B flat major, the last for both groups in C major. The roaring boys sing of the pleasures of motiveless violence, the whores of the delights of gainful seduction, and at the end they propose a toast to their respective commanders, Mars and Venus.
Recitative and scene. 'Come, Tom.' Shadow and Mother Goose catechise Tom in the philosophy of the selfish pursuit of pleasure. He replies correctly that the aim of existence is to do one's duty to oneself (C major), that Nature must be the only moral guide (D flat major), that Nature holds the secret of Beauty (C major), that Beauty is the transitory source of pleasure (D major), that pleasure is the gratification of dreams (D major – C major). Only when Shadow asks him to define Love does he falter in his answer, and, remembering the power of the emotion, he gives vent to his feeling in an agitated mezza voce aside, accompanied by an intimate but highly charged ensemble of flutes, clarinet and solo string quintet. The irregularity of this short passage of arioso is further heightened by the key of E flat minor: Tom is now far removed indeed from the A major of the opening pastoral. And he recognises the fact. He responds violently to Shadow's encouragement and Mother Goose's offer of wine. Then, as a cuckoo clock coos one, he asks to go before it is too late. But Shadow simply has the clock turn back, and it sounds twelve to an arpeggio in B flat climbing down through the wind. 'Time is yours', he tells his master, the present is for pleasure.

Chorus. 'Soon dawn will glitter.' In two stanzas, both sung to the same music in B flat major, the whores and roaring boys sing beguilingly of enjoying oneself while opportunity offers.
Recitative [secco]. 'Sisters of Venus, Brothers of Mars'. Shadow introduces Tom to the company to sing a song.
Cavatina. 'Love, too frequently betrayed'. Tom laments his betrayal of Love and passionately begs that the goddess will not abandon him. The cavatina, properly cast in two stanzas, is accompanied in the main by strings and a prominent clarinet, and is in the key of C sharp minor (though Tom leans on the dominant). Thus, like Tom's earlier reference to Love in this scene, the passage is removed tonally from its surroundings, but there is more to it than that. In using E flat minor he showed how far he was from his union with Anne; in now calling upon C sharp minor he shows how far he is from the G major of himself at the start of the opera.
Chorus. 'How sad a song'. Spellbound and charmed by Tom's melancholy song, the whores remain in its key of C sharp minor. But then Mother Goose pushes them aside with a decisive chord of D major, and cadences equally firmly in G major as she claims Tom for herself for the night.
Chorus. 'The sun is bright, the grass is green; Lanterloo, lanterloo.' This big, swaying 6/8 chorus brings the scene to an end in the key of A major once more. But the homecoming is ironic. The country reed ensemble is expanded to an urban serenade band of oboes, clarinets, bassoons and horns in pairs, sounding a ritornello, and the innocence of the opera's beginning is quite gone. At first the whores and roaring boys seem to be singing a nursery-rhyme nocturne, but then, as they reach out from A major to B, D, G and C, their words become more mysterious and sexually suggestive. In a parody of children's May Day ceremonial they conduct Tom and Mother Goose to bed, leaving Shadow alone to wish his master sweet dreams, with the warning that when he wakes he dies.

Scene 3

As scene 1, but under a moonlit autumn night.
[Introduction]. A trio of oboe, cor anglais and bassoon recalls the introduction to the first scene, but the key is now A minor and the atmosphere poignant.
Recitative. 'No word from Tom', with reed trio and strings. Anne, who has this scene exclusively to herself, enters from the house in travelling clothes. She has had no word from Tom, and so determines that he must be in difficulty and need her help. She will go to him. The key of her recitative is the A minor of the introduction.

Aria. 'Quietly, night'. In two similar stanzas she calls on the night to find and caress Tom's heart, and on the moon to guide her and shine also on him. She is accompanied principally by the strings and an obbligato bassoon in free canon with her; the key is B minor.

Recitative. 'My father!', with orchestra. She hears her father calling her from within the house, and for a moment she makes to return. But she decides that Tom's weakness makes his need the greater. She asks God to protect her father and strengthen her resolve.

Cabaletta. 'I go to him.' Completing a further rise to the decisive key of C major, the scene ends with a grand, resilient number in which Anne declares that true love cannot alter or be shifted. She has a floridly decorated da capo, concluding on a high C, and the curtain comes down quickly as she turns to leave by the garden gate.

Act II

Scene 1

The morning room of Tom's house in London. He is seated alone at the breakfast table on a bright day.

[Introduction]. A short orchestral passage, beginning in D and preparing for the aria which follows.

Aria. 'Vary the song.' Tom complains mournfully that all the variety of London cannot fill the gap that remains in his heart, a gap sustained in the music, which hovers between B flat major and its relative minor, G. The choice is of course not accidental: G has been Tom's since the first number, and B flat major has been the key of his wishes realised (compare the quartet in Act I scene 1 and the clock episode of scene 2). In hovering between the two he is torn between what he is and what he would be: the mood of troubled, dawning self-realisation is not dissimilar to that of Oedipus's aria 'Invidia fortunam odit', likewise undecided between E flat major and C minor.

Recitative. 'O Nature, green unnatural mother', with orchestra. Tom regrets his move from the country to the city, where one must be a slave to fashion. He has no appetite left for strange foods, wines and cards (A flat major, with horn solo), nor for women: only one is honest, chaste and kind, and of her he dare not think (though he has done so in having this section rise a semitone to A minor, the key of her opening recitative in the preceding scene; the horn solo is replaced by one for trumpet). With a further semitone rise to B flat minor, and in a new dynamic tempo, Tom calls Nature to the hunt: he has no course but to pursue his appetites.

Aria (reprise). 'Always the quarry'. In a varied repeat of 'Vary the song', with the same tonal ambiguity, Tom laments his inability to find what he most longs for, laments the emptiness of his present life. After a short postlude for strings he makes his second wish: 'I wish I were happy.'

Recitative [secco]. 'Master, are you alone?' Shadow again appears in answer to his wish, carrying a broadsheet. He shows it to Tom, who recognises it as referring to Baba the Turk, a sideshow at St Giles's Fair (why she is appearing there we do not yet know). He asks Tom whether he desires her or is obliged to her: the answer to both is a firm negative. Therefore, since he is bound neither by wish nor by conscience, Shadow suggests he should marry Baba, and he develops his reasoning in a passage of arioso accompanied by pattering semiquavers in the strings. The mass of men, he observes, are in a condition of wretched slavery either to desire or to duty. If Tom is to be free, then he must ignore both. Returning to recitative, Shadow asks his master to consider Baba's picture and his words.

Aria. 'In youth the panting slave'. Shadow takes up the key of Tom's longings, B flat major, and tells him how men are commonly enslaved by sexual attraction in youth, worldly advancement in middle life and moral virtue in old age. In the slower middle section of his number, beginning in unabashed C major, he declares that the only free man is he who makes his own decisions and 'wills his choice as destiny' (again a sinister high E on this last word). Then, with a return to his opening manner, he tells Tom that he will be answerable only to himself if he can free himself from Passion's compulsion and Reason's restraint.

Duet–finale. 'My tale shall be told.' The emphatic G major chords at the start of this number indicate Tom's enthusiastic acceptance of Shadow's ideas. The two join in a big gigue-like duet which stays rooted in G major to the end: Tom is now persuaded of what he must do, and all the doubts of his aria at the beginning of the scene have been dispelled, taking with them the emergent self-knowledge. He says how his exploit in winning Baba will make him famous for evermore; meanwhile Shadow busies himself with preparing his master as a 'bachelor of fashion'. Finally the two join together in exultation and mock gravity, calling on heavenly powers to guide Tom to 'Hymen's Altar', and the piece ends with a peroration of brisk orchestral chords.

Scene 2

The street before Tom's London house at dusk in autumn. The entrance is in the centre of the stage.

[Introduction]. The scene is set by the orchestra in dark C minor, with a pathetic trumpet solo. Anne comes on and goes to knock at the door, but she stops and hides when she sees a servant coming out from the servants' entrance. Only when he has gone does she step forward.

Recitative and arioso. 'How strange!' Her opening recitative with strings, remaining in C minor, finds her frightened and alone but propelled by her love for Tom. In arioso and in B minor she calls on her heart to be stronger and give her the courage to win Tom back: the feeling and the key recall her aria 'Quietly, night' in Act I scene 3, since which scene, of course, she has not been seen. But the larger part of the number is in E flat major, in which key she gathers her strength, and in its relative minor. 'A love that is sworn before Thee', she declares to Heaven, 'can plunder Hell of its prey.' Then, with a shift to F major, servants come on to a 2/4 march scored for a classical orchestra of oboes, horns and strings (though sporting a characteristically Stravinskyan trio for violas in its middle section). The servants carry into the house a variety of strange wrapped packages, and Anne wonders what can be afoot: intuitively she realises that it cannot be good. At the end of the procession comes a sedan chair, from which Tom steps out. She recognises him at once.

Duet. 'Anne! here!' Anne rushes to Tom, but he holds her away from him, startled to see her. They sing in a distraught F minor (F major was the key of their rapturous duet in the middle of the Act I scene 1 quartet), he advising her to denounce him and leave, she saying she cannot and asking quietly 'Do you return?' At the mention of this fateful word 'return' Tom is violently taken aback, and Anne too says that she cannot go back if he will not. Then singing together, but in separate asides, he wishes the word 'return' obliterated and she prays for help to calm him. Tom collects his thoughts and the number moves into its slower middle section, in C minor: he tries to persuade her by telling her that London is no place for genuine virtue, but she says that she need not fear when she has his aid and her love to help her. The suggestion that he may be of some use to Anne brings a return to the F minor music: no, he says, London has corrupted him, and she must go back. She replies that his worthiness is of no account; it matters only that he still loves her. He is touched and moves towards her.

Recitative. 'My Love, am I to remain in here forever?' Baba interrupts the long duet with an address to her new husband: he must help her from the sedan or fear the consequences. Her little arioso, absurdly featuring a pair of bassoons, is in D major, already established as her key in the dry recitative of Act II scene 1 where Tom and Shadow discussed her for the first time. She then goes on in recitative to ask Tom

Synopsis

to finish his business with whoever is detaining him. Anne is confused; Tom explains that he is now married; and Anne remarks with slight bitterness that she must have been the unworthy one.

Trio. 'Could it then have been known?' In parallel verses Anne and Tom comment on what has happened: she considers the folly of swearing love when one may so easily be deceived, while he laments that he is now cut off from love for ever. They come together at two significant points, first on the word 'never', in roulades which promise to cadence and do not, and then finally in minor thirds on the words 'For ever'. The third voice is that of Baba, who expresses her irritation in her own quicker tempo. The key is E minor with a pull towards the relative major, except for a passage in E flat minor, where Tom calls passionately for any hope of love to be gone, and remembers the key of his appalled apostrophe to Love in the Brothel scene. At the end of the ensemble Anne leaves.

Finale. 'I have not run away, dear heart.' A grand sarabande in D major is sounded by oboes, trumpets, horns and string nonet. Baba says that she is still waiting, and Tom helps her from the sedan. She asks him who it was detaining him: only a milkmaid, he says. Then the full orchestra joins in the sarabande, together with a chorus of townspeople who come onto the stage to welcome Baba to her new home. The couple go up the steps to the house. Tom enters, but Baba turns to the admiring crowd, revealing her full black beard. She blows them a kiss and stands with arms outstretched as the curtain falls and the orchestra sweeps majestically to a close.

Scene 3

As Act II scene 1, but the room is now cluttered up with curiosities.

Aria. 'As I was saying'. After a preamble for clarinets and strings the curtain rises to reveal Tom and Baba at breakfast, he sulking, she seemingly discovered in the middle of a monologue. She joins the busy orchestra, chattering away in F major about her former admirers and the presents they gave her, these being the objects that fill the room. She stops to remark that Tom is not eating, but then immediately continues as before. She stops again to ask him what is the matter, but he answers her in a surly manner.

Baba's song. 'Come, sweet, come.' She tries to coax him round by singing a little unaccompanied ditty. He pushes her away and tells her to sit down.

Aria. 'Scorned! Abused!' Baba now launches at once into a powerful dramatic aria in D minor. In two similar stanzas she vents her fury at

Tom's neglect of her and also her jealousy of Anne. She picks up things and smashes them to the ground. She presses her face into his. Finally Tom can stand it no longer. He takes his wig and plops it down on her head, back to front, cutting her off in the middle of a cadential run on the word 'never': once more, but now bathetically, 'never' is left proceeding into endlessness.

Recitative. 'My heart is cold', with strings and horn. Baba remains in her place. Tom walks about the room and then flings himself down on a sofa to sleep. His short monologue establishes the key of the next number, G major.

Pantomime. Shadow wheels in a 'phantastic baroque machine', graphically depicted in shrill, circling music for flute and piccolo (an instrument used only in this machine music). He demonstrates to the audience the trickery by which the machine is made to seem to convert a broken piece of vase into a loaf of bread, and as he does so he sings lightheartedly to himself.

Recitative–arioso–recitative. 'O I wish it were true.' Tom makes the third of his spoken wishes, and again he finds Shadow before him. In excited arioso, in E major, he tells Shadow how he dreamed he had invented a machine to make bread from stones and so abolish want, make the earth an Eden. The machine music returns, decelerated, and with it the key of G major. Shadow shows his own machine and asks whether Tom's resembled it: they are, of course, identical, and Tom is able to put the machine through its paces. He sinks to his knees and prays, in his aspirational key of B flat major, that his invention may make him at last worthy of Anne.

Duet. 'Thanks to this excellent device'. In buoyant E flat major Tom voices his hope that the new machine will create again Heaven on earth, bringing Man to dominion over Nature. He has three stanzas in this vein, forming the 'A' sections of an A–B–A–B–A form. The 'B' sections, in foreign keys, belong to Shadow, who addresses the audience directly: they can see that his master is a fool, but the venture is sure to be profitable, and so investments are warmly invited. The last section of the duet has the two together, at divergent purposes still.

Recitative. 'Forgive me, master.' In dry recitative Shadow interrupts Tom's rapture to point out that the business of advertisement and manufacture still has to be considered. Tom recognises the truth of this and is downcast, for it is impossible that anyone of probity should trust such a one as him. But Shadow says that he has already taken the matter in hand and found some potential backers. The vigorous E flat major music of the duet returns, and the two begin to wheel the machine

Synopsis

away. However, before they leave Shadow suggests that perhaps Tom should tell his wife the good news. No, says Tom, he has no wife: he's buried her. (On the surface this is a joke at the expense of the bewigged Baba, but it also touches more keenly on his most passionate line from the trio in the previous scene: 'O bury the heart there deeper than it sound.')

Act III

Scene 1

As the last, but everything is now dusty and neglected. Baba is still in her place. It is a spring afternoon.
Introduction and chorus. 'Ruin. Disaster. Shame'. There is a lively orchestral introduction which in its key, E major, and its tempo recalls the Prelude to the opera. But the first three words of the chorus, heard from behind the curtain and sung in B minor, indicate that Tom's commercial venture has not been a success. The curtain rises to show solid citizens examining the contents of his house in preparation for an auction. The music returns to E major, with a typical strong suggestion of the dominant, as the chorus of prospective buyers rub their hands over Tom's downfall and their own opportunity to profit from it. They then reflect on the vicissitudes of fate, which can bring about the ruin even of sober merchants and duchesses, and here the key is B flat major tending towards G minor, as in Tom's aria at the start of Act II scene 1. The effect, however, is reversed. The chorus sings with the voice of respectable society condemning the hapless individual: they range themselves on either side of the 'gap' which Tom had expressed. Next, with a return to E major and to the opening tempo, Anne comes in and asks where Tom is: reports differ, but the chorus is sure he is in debt and pursued by the authorities. Anne goes off to look for him, and then rising excitement in the orchestra prepares for the entrance of Sellem, the auctioneer. He immediately takes charge; the crowd is awestruck.
Recitative. 'Ladies, both fair and gracious', with orchestra. He welcomes everyone to the sale and muses on the nature of auctions, which he sees as divine instruments for the preservation of natural order: 'a thousand lose that a thousand may gain'. Then he introduces the first lots.
Aria. 'Who hears me, knows me.' Sellem encourages the bidding for a stuffed auk and a mounted fish. He sings in F major, a key recalling Baba's breathless aria at the start of the preceding scene, as does the accompanying rapid stutter of repeated notes in the trumpets: it is of

course Baba's collection, described in that earlier aria, which is being sold. There is a shift to G major for the start of the bidding.
Bidding scene. 'Seven, seven'. In a little C major episode the sale is concluded.
Aria (continuing). 'Behold it.' Almost exactly as before Sellem excites interest in a new range of objects: a marble bust, a palm branch and other things unspecified.
Bidding scene. 'Fifteen, fifteen'. Again as before.
Recitative [secco]. 'Wonderful'. Sellem briefly prepares the crowd for something really novel.
Aria (continued). 'An unknown object draws us.' The final section of Sellem's aria is by contrast with the others slow and expectant, and in E flat major, though the bidding begins as before in G major. The 'unknown object' is the covered Baba.
Final bidding scene. 'Fifty, fifty'. The bidding is now much more enthusiastic, starting out from D instead of C, and at the end, as he shouts 'Gone', Sellem has to quieten the crowd by a dramatic gesture: he pulls the wig from Baba's head, and she finishes the run that had been interrupted.
Aria. 'Sold! Annoyed!' Indignantly she continues with a third stanza to her D minor aria, furious this time with the crowd, whom she insists must go. When she has finished there is a sharp disjunction, marked tonally, scenically and in terms of colour: Tom and Shadow are heard from off stage in a street-cry, 'Old wives for sale', Tom chanting on E flat and Shadow on A flat, without accompaniment.
Recitative. 'Now what was that?', with orchestra. Fascinated by the interruption, and by its tonality, the crowd wonders what is happening. Baba, however, recognises both her betrayers and Anne, who rushes onto the stage. She calls the 'milkmaid' to her; Sellem asks them both to withdraw so that the auction can continue; but the crowd would rather play voyeur.
Duet. 'You love him.' Baba tells Anne that she can still rescue Tom, since he still loves her (C major). Anne expresses her delight and blames only herself for ever doubting him (F major), while Sellem and the crowd try to work out what is going on. With a return to the opening music of the number, Baba encourages Anne to go and find Tom; as for herself, she need not fear the future. Proudly in A flat major, accompanied by horn and strings, she declares that she will go back to the stage: her new tonic, diametrically opposed to her previous D, suggests that she has found a new, true home after her flamboyant excursion into married life. And as an artist, unlike the other characters in the opera, she holds it in her power to return. The final section of

the ensemble, back in F major, has Anne wondering scrupulously whether she can happily love Tom and also believe Baba happy without him, while Baba repeats her determination to return to her natural element, the crowd observes with keen interest and Sellem laments the foundered auction.

Ballad tune. 'If boys had wings'. Tom and Shadow are heard again from the street, now singing a nonsense rhyme in B flat major, the key of Tom's wish for escape: by this point escape can only be into insanity. The strangeness of the interruption is enhanced by the simple arpeggio accompaniment for horns, timpani and pizzicato low strings, in decisive contrast with the clamour of soloists, chorus and orchestra in recognising the unseen singers once their little song is over.

Stretto–finale. 'I go to him.' Anne resolves to go to Tom and summons her strength anew: the principal keys are C minor and its relative major, as in her number of similar determination at the start of Act II scene 2. Baba gives her further encouragement and a blessing, and Sellem and the chorus also join in to hasten her on her way. She rushes off.

Ballad tune (reprise). 'Who cares a fig?' Tom and Shadow sing another rhyme as they disappear into the distance, the piece shortened and with clarinet replacing horn.

[Finale continued]. 'You! Summon my carriage!' Baba imperiously calls on Sellem to prepare for her departure, and he is too stunned to do other than obey. She makes her exit, telling the crowd that the next time they see her they will have to pay, and the mob is at last bemused by so much excitement. The E major music is that of the scene's opening.

Scene 2

A churchyard with a newly dug grave under a starless night sky.

Prelude. A slow, highly chromatic page for solo string quartet takes a dark and tortuous path from a vague B flat minor to a surer F major, at which the curtain rises and Tom and Shadow enter.

Duet. 'How dark and dreadful is this place.' Tom expresses his fearfulness, not only of the place but also of Shadow's countenance. Each of his little couplets is introduced by a ritornello for flutes and clarinet that will become important as the opera moves now to its end, and the floridity of his line, coupled with the key of G minor, recalls that of his aria 'Vary the song', though in this weak, bleak music there is no hint of the major mode. Shadow, however, is quite at home here. He sings in G major, to a near variant of the ballad tune, that it is now time for him to collect his wages. Tom returns to his G minor music, without the ritornello, and tells his servant that he must be patient until his master is a rich man again. Shadow too has a second stanza, in the G major of which he has already taken possession from Tom; he informs Tom that he wants not his money but his soul, and invites him to look into his eyes and recognise who his servant is. With dramatic emphasis he moves into B minor and invites Tom to look at his waiting grave. He must choose now the manner of his dying. Tom comes back once more in G minor but now in a more anguished manner to call on the hills or seas to cover him, and Shadow joins him to repeat the message of hopelessness. The music slows down again for a little interlude played by oboes and bassoons, after which Shadow announces in B minor that midnight has come and with it Tom's time to kill himself. An off-stage bell, tuned to F, sounds nine strokes, but then in answer to Tom's plea for mercy Shadow stops the clock again.

Recitative [secco]. 'Very well'. With a brightening shift to B major, Shadow relents and becomes his old charming self. He proposes a game of chance to decide Tom's fate. They will use the pack of cards that is Tom's last possession: Shadow will cut three cards, and if Tom can name them he will go free; if not he must follow his old servant. Tom nods his agreement to the terms.

Duet. 'Well, then'. The game proceeds in a long number of which a large part is accompanied only by the harpsichord. There is a weird, creeping superimposition of major and minor keys, chiefly F sharp minor with F major, while Tom expresses his fearfulness. Shadow gives him a clue to the first card: he must think of someone he would rather have running the game. Naturally Tom thinks of Anne and names the Queen of Hearts, correctly. The oppressive harpsichord music is cut off, and the clock strikes once more. Shadow turns to address the audience, pointing out that one success will encourage Tom's hopes and so make his eventual despair all the greater (A minor). The second round is a variation of the first. Tom is again troubled, and Shadow says he must trust in Fortune as once he did. A spade falls, and Tom in his alarm automatically cries out: 'The deuce!' Thus he comes calmly to recognise what the card must be: the two of Spades. Again the accompaniment stops and the clock strikes. But then, at the point where Shadow had earlier turned to the audience, he warns Tom in recitative that his next choice is the last and most crucial. Tom wonders passionately what hope he can possibly have at this stage, and his voice brings a brief, comforting entry from the woodwind for the first time in the number. Now Shadow turns to the audience and, in F Lydian, shows them how he intends to trick Tom by cutting again the Queen of Hearts, to be for him the 'Queen of Hell' (again the high E on this last word). He invites

Synopsis

Tom to make his choice, and there follows a short duet in which Tom asks whether Fortune will give him another sign and Shadow says it will not: there is a key signature of three flats but no stable tonality, until the final B minor of Shadow's insistence that Tom decide, a return to the key of his devilish pronouncements earlier in the scene. Tom recognises a track of cloven hooves, which Shadow sardonically shrugs off as left by goats enjoying the fresh greenery of 'spring's return'. The word 'return' excites Tom to an outburst of tormented feeling in which he calls for Love to return, and he is answered by Anne off stage singing the key phrase of her arioso in Act II scene 2, 'A Love that is sworn before thee', in its original C minor. Then Tom makes his fourth and last spoken wish, this time preceded by a flourish in the harpsichord: 'I wish for nothing else.' At last sure of himself, singing in C major with firm string accompaniment, Tom calls on Love to 'assume eternal reign'. He names the Queen of Hearts again; the bell sounds its twelfth stroke; and he sinks to the ground. Shadow then has a dramatic B flat minor aria in two short stanzas as he feels the nearness of Hell, and in a final section he curses Tom with insanity, once more emphasising his high E, which sounds especially chilling in the present tonal context. There is an orchestral postlude with trumpet solo, and then the woodwind ritornello from the beginning of the scene returns, scored now for flute, oboe and clarinet, extended, and in the relative major: B flat. The fact that this has always been the key of Tom's hopes makes it all the more touching that he should be discovered here bereft of his wits. Dawn breaks on a spring morning, and he is sitting on a mound over the covered grave, singing to the ballad tune that he is Adonis. The woodwind trio close the scene.

Scene 3

Bedlam. Tom faces a group of madmen.
[Introduction]. Flutes, clarinets and strings set the scene in A major music which recalls, as from another world, the pastoral tone of the first scene.
Arioso. 'Prepare yourselves, heroic shades.' In the same key Tom calls the denizens of the madhouse to wash, anoint and dress themselves for the arrival of Venus to visit her Adonis; the wan orchestration of the introduction is continued.
Dialogue. 'Madmen's words are all untrue.' Still in A major, the chorus of madmen declare – while throwing doubt on their veracity in their first line – that Venus will not come, but Tom insists that she will.

Chorus-minuet. 'Leave all hope and love behind.' The madmen, accompanied by the full orchestra, dance before Tom and mock him, singing of their condition while circling into and out of C major. That key – coupled with the fact that this is the first choral song, properly speaking, since Act I scene 2 – may remind one of the chorus of roaring boys and whores at the start of that scene. The atmosphere is of course very different, flat where the earlier number was thoroughly dynamic, but this is again a chorus of statement on behalf of a particular section aside from normal society. The madmen sing that they are without love or hope, ignored and changeless, expressing all this without bitterness or rhetoric. They have four stanzas, separated by brief interludes for oboe, viola and bassoons, the last stanza extended and followed by a short passage in which they recognise the arrival of the Keeper as Minos.
Recitative [secco]. 'There he is.' The Keeper of the Madhouse brings Anne in and explains to her that Tom will answer only to the name of Adonis. He leaves them together, and, prompted by a clarinet, Anne addresses Tom under his mythological name. Adonis duly recognises his Venus, joined by flutes and clarinets in E flat major, which was the key of Tom's totally unrealistic optimism at the end of Act II.
Arioso. 'I have waited.' In the same key Tom rejoices that he has at last been vindicated, and then, against broad chords played by oboes, clarinets and horns in G major, he leads Venus to mount his pallet as her throne and hear the confession of his sins.
Duet. 'In a foolish dream'. Tom returns to the tonality of his mad song at the end of the preceding scene: a B flat major in which he lingers on the mediant (the shadows of G minor, mingled with this key in such earlier numbers as his aria 'Vary the song', are now clearly separated into the woodwind parts). Though insane, he sees that he has erred by disdaining Venus's love, and he asks her for forgiveness. She answers that the past is transfigured by his penitence, and then he asks her to embrace him as the returning prodigal. In a coda they sing together, taking up the woodwind ritornello from the opening and closing of the previous scene, and echoing the madmen in finding here no difference of space or time, no 'notion of Almost or Too Late'.
Recitative quasi arioso. 'I am exceeding weary', with strings. Still in B flat, Tom sings that he is tired. He lays his head on her breast and asks her to sing him to sleep.
Lullaby. 'Gently, little boat'. Anne sings a lullaby in three stanzas, in A flat major (the comforting key of Baba's return to her true home), accompanied by the flutes. Each stanza is answered by the madmen, who are alternately soothed (in B flat minor) and elated (in B major) by Anne's song.

Synopsis

Recitative [secco]. 'Anne, my dear'. The Keeper comes back with Trulove, who calls his daughter to come home now (to E major, the key of the opera's opening). She answers in agreement, looks back to Tom and bids him farewell in his key of B flat major.

Duettino. 'Every wearied body must'. A counterpart to the duettino of the first scene, in the same key of G major, this number has Anne and her father retiring from Tom and expressing their sorrow.

Finale: recitative and chorus. 'Where art thou, Venus?' Tom wakes and looks round in agitation for his Venus. The first part of his recitative remains in the flat keys that dominate this scene, particularly A flat, while the accompaniment features a solo string quartet again, a woodwind quartet and eventually the full string orchestra. Shouting he calls for his courtiers, Achilles, Helen and the rest, then demands from the madmen where they have hidden his Venus. They answer that no-one has been there, at which Tom's heart breaks and he feels the approach of death. He has a last song, floridly decorated, in which he asks Orpheus to strike up a dirge and calls on nymphs and shepherds to weep for Adonis.

Mourning chorus. 'Mourn for Adonis.' In A minor, solemnly accompanied by low woodwind, brass, timpani and low strings, the madmen sing their lament. The number ends with three A minor chords deep in bassoons, brass and timpani.

Epilogue

'Good people, just a moment'. The mood is suddenly switched by a bright chord of A major played by the full orchestra, launching the Epilogue in the same 2/4 time of the mourning chorus but at double the speed. In front of the curtain, and with the house lights up, the five principals come on without their wigs or, in the case of Baba, beard. In chorus they ask the audience to wait a while, since there is still the moral to be drawn from the story just ended. Anne warns that not every rake is rescued by Love from Duty, and she is followed in matching stanzas by Baba, who advises the ladies that all men are mad and actors, by Tom, echoed by Trulove, with the message to young men not to think too grandly of themselves, and by Shadow, who sings humorously of his lamentable existence: he must do as he is told, while not being believed in. Finally they join together again in their last stricture:

> For idle hands
> And hearts and minds
> The Devil finds
> A work to do.

5 Performance history

The Rake's Progress was embarked upon with no practical incentive, which was most unusual for Stravinsky: very nearly all of his major works were commissioned, or written with a definite prospect of performance (in the case of his scores for Dyagilev), or composed to provide a performing repertory for himself. He was thus quite unused to the problems of placing a work, and when he got around to considering the matter it seems his first thought was that his opera might receive its première in the United States, perhaps enjoying a run in a small New York theatre as Menotti's *The Consul* did in 1950.[1] During that year the possibility was raised with several potential backers, but finance was not forthcoming, any more than for Tom's Bread Machine. However, definite interest in the work was shown by David Webster on behalf of Covent Garden and by Carl Ebert and Raymond Kendall on behalf of the University of Southern California Opera Department.[2]

Either of these would have been natural venues for the opera's first performance: London because much of the action takes place there, Los Angeles because it was Stravinsky's home. But the composer's wish that the work be presented in a small theatre – plus the promise of a $20,000 commissioning fee from the Italian government – was enough to make him decide in favour of the Biennale di Venezia, who would give the première in the Teatro La Fenice as the star attraction of their fourteenth international festival of contemporary music. No doubt the choice was influenced too by Stravinsky's affection for Venice and his previous successes at the festival there, where in 1925 he had played his Piano Sonata in the Fenice. So it was that, following even in this the example of Mozart with a certain twist, *The Rake's Progress* was given for the first time in a country not sharing its language.

Negotiations with Venice, which had been conducted through Nicholas Nabokov, were not concluded until Stravinsky signed a contract on 6 February 1951,[3] with the performance scheduled to take place in the following September. Practical arrangements had, therefore, to be made in great haste. Stravinsky had agreed to conduct the first performance himself, and he swiftly secured a producer in Carl Ebert, whom he chose because, as he wrote to an uncertain Auden, 'he is an experienced musician and also he is already familiar with my score'.[4] But other details were decided only at the last minute. Not until July did La Scala assume responsibility for the production,[5] and it was also not till that month that singers, designers and an assistant conductor began to be engaged. As designer Stravinsky had wanted Eugene Berman, Russian-born and a close friend at the time (in 1944 he had been responsible for the striking designs for the first ballet production of *Danses concertantes*). Stravinsky had settled on Berman as early as January 1949,[6] but in the event the artist was not available, nor was the composer's second choice, John Piper, and so he had to content himself with two Italians, Gianni Ratto for the sets and Ebe Colciaghi for the costumes. As his conducting deputy, to take rehearsals and direct the second and third performances, Stravinsky originally wanted Igor Markevich,[7] but he proved unacceptable to the Italians and Ferdinand Leitner was chosen. The cast so hurriedly assembled was as follows: Robert Rounseville (Tom), Elisabeth Schwarzkopf (Anne), Otakar Kraus (Shadow), Jennie Tourel (Baba), Rafael Ariè (Trulove), Nell Tangeman (Mother Goose), Hugues Cuenod (Sellem) and Emanuel Menkes (Keeper of the Madhouse).

The première, on 11 September 1951, was an occasion whose glamour, sparkle and excitement have been well described by Robert Craft[8] and Vera Stravinsky,[9] both of whom speak more of its social éclat than of its musical and dramatic achievements, perhaps because these were less remarkable. Rounseville, 'only recently emerged, or not quite fully emerged', according to Vera Stravinsky, 'from a film career and manner', was generally found quite inadequate in the central role, and Tourel was miscast as a 'delicate miniature', to quote Lord Harewood,[10] of a bearded woman. Auden's view, shared by other observers more disinterested, was that the sets were un-English and the production weak.[11] And Stravinsky's conducting was found to be much less sure and pointed than that of Leitner. Only Schwarzkopf, Kraus and Cuenod appear to have come out of the performance with credit, and they were all retained in their roles when the production was revived on its home ground, at La Scala, in the following December. Leitner then conducted all four performances, and the new principals were Mirto Picchi as Tom and Cloè Elmo as Baba. The opera was given in Italian, as *Carriera d'un libertino*, which must have reduced the problems the Milanese chorus had originally experienced with the text. After that the première production was never seen again, and indeed La Scala did not revive the work they had introduced until 1979, when they imported the London Sinfonietta to play the score.

Despite its inauspicious début, and despite the misgivings of critics who, like Colin Mason, thought the libretto clumsy and particularly poor in its handling of Baba (this was to remain a common complaint),[12] the opera was quickly and widely taken up by other houses. Nor is this surprising. With the death of Schoenberg — just while the hectic preparations for the première were getting under way, on 13 July 1951 — Stravinsky was now indisputably the outstanding composer of the age, and *The Rake's Progress* was his only full-length opera and by far his biggest single work. In 1952 it was given in Vienna, Geneva, Strasbourg and several German towns. In 1953 it received its first performance in Paris, at the Opéra-Comique (18 June, conducted by André Cluytens and produced by Louis Musy), and its British première in the form of a BBC studio recording for radio (broadcast on 2 January, conducted by Paul Sacher and produced by Dennis Arundell). The first staging in Britain followed on 25 August of the same year at the Edinburgh Festival, in a production by Glyndebourne Festival Opera which gave Carl Ebert the opportunity to achieve a more settled and successful presentation, helped by Osbert Lancaster's sets and costumes. The conductor was Alfred Wallenstein, then musical director of the Los Angeles Philharmonic, and the cast included Richard Lewis as Tom, Jerome Hines as Shadow, Elsie Morison as Anne and Nan Merriman as Baba.

During 1953 there were also two productions in the United States in which Stravinsky was involved. The American première took place at the Metropolitan Opera in New York on St Valentine's Day, conducted by Fritz Reiner, produced by the composer's long-standing friend and collaborator George Balanchine, and designed by Horace Armistead. The cast, which Stravinsky had helped select after hearing in the same house a performance of *Cosi fan tutte*,[13] was led by Eugene Conley as Tom, Hilde Gueden as Anne, Mack Harrell as Shadow and Blanche Thebom as Baba. In March the same performers moved into the Columbia studios in order to make the first commercial recording of the opera, for which Stravinsky took over the baton, and for which he secured orchestral forces more to his liking than those that had been deemed appropriate in the theatre, where the work had been given with quintuple wind and piano instead of harpsichord.[14] Then in May he conducted the opera again, this time for the Boston University Opera Workshop, directed by Sarah Caldwell (Robert Craft was engaged as assistant producer). And this was a significant event, for it proved that the piece was one that students could tackle.

Performance history

The lesson was well noted. The first staging in England was owed to the Cambridge University Opera Group, who gave the opera on 19 December 1956 in a production by Brian Trowell conducted by Leon Lovett, with Kenneth Bowen as the Rake and Raymond Hayter his Shadow. All four of these Cambridge participants were assembled again when the work received its London stage première, given under the auspices of the New Opera Company at Sadler's Wells Theatre on 22 July 1957, just four days after Robert Craft had conducted the opera for the first time, in a new production at Santa Fe (his Rake was Loren Driscoll, who later sang the role in Hamburg and Berlin). That same summer also saw the Dutch première, by the Netherlands Opera in a Holland Festival production at the Hague (17 June), when the conductor was Erich Leinsdorf, the producer Peter Potter and the leading men the well-experienced Conley and Kraus.

The next landmark in the stage history of the opera, a major one, was the production by Ingmar Bergman mounted in Stockholm by the Royal Swedish Opera, which opened on 22 April 1961 and proved a great public success. The conductor was Michael Gielen, the designers Berger Bergling (sets) and Kerstin Hedeby (costumes), and the cast included Ragnar Ulfung as Tom, Margareta Hallin as Anne, Erik Saedén as Shadow and Kerstin Meyer as Baba. (Excerpts from the opera were later commercially recorded by Ulfung and Hallin; see Discography.) Stravinsky saw the production in September, with Craft, who reported in his diary that he had 'never seen I.S. more moved by a performance of a work of his — in fact, one seldom sees him not angry — and this in spite of impossible musical cuts, bad *tempi*, and legions of places where the direction is at loggerheads with the book'.[15]

Bergman followed what had very quickly become the composer's own preference in giving the opera with a single interval, after Act II scene 2: this was the practice adopted at the first Metropolitan performances and also at Glyndebourne. The Swedish director's reasons, however, were his own. As he told Stravinsky and Craft, he found this division of the work produced two strongly continuous units, 'protasis' and 'peripateia',[16] and he justified his cuts as helping to achieve the same end of concentrating the audience's attention.[17] The whole point was to present the opera as a crucially important and directly meaningful experience, and yet at the same time as a fable. The stage was thrust forward over part of the pit; there was no curtain, only what Craft described as 'a Brechtian poster'[18] dropped down between episodes; and the grey settings, 'suggesting the engravings of Hogarth' according to one report,[19] were manoeuvred in full view of the audience and often with the characters already in place. But along with these aliena-

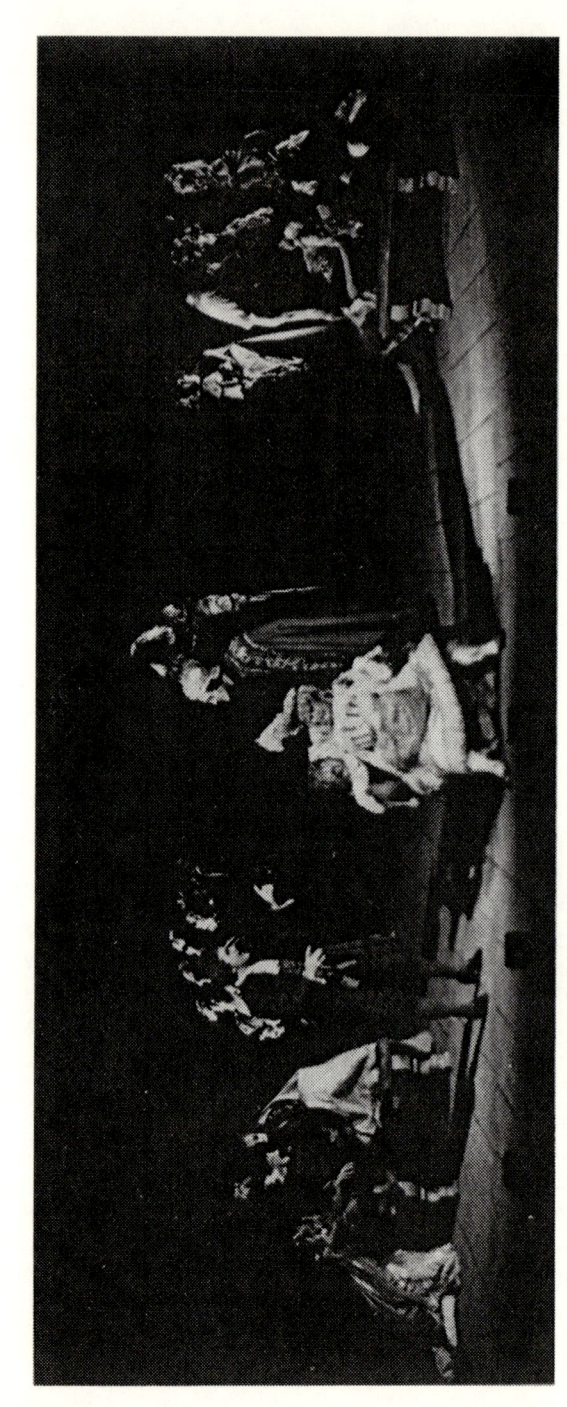

10 Stockholm 1961: the Brothel scene

11 Stockholm 1961: the Auction scene

tion devices went a close concern to give powerful expression to details of personality, relationship and motivation. Craft recalls Stravinsky praising such attentions in the following terms: 'Anne weeps when Tom leaves for London, and Tom starts to go to her, but Trulove motions him back and goes to her himself. I cannot describe Trulove's gesture, but I believed in it. Also, Tom and Shadow singing from the loges in the auction scene *does* bolster the idea that they are at large. Such small things, and a hundred more, establish the credibility of the play.'[20]

One may note here a feeling of gratitude that Bergman had thoroughly vindicated the composer's decision to set a libretto that had been widely criticised as trivial, inconsistent and unbelievable. Naturally, therefore, Stravinsky particularly applauded the director's achievement in making Baba for once real and sympathetic, not just a grotesque but a personification, for Bergman, of the artist in everyone.[21] Artists, though, as Bergman well knew, are by no means similar creatures, and his production gained an essential edge from his recognition of the gulf separating the 'artistic moralist' Hogarth from the 'religious moralist' Stravinsky.[22] (It is worth noting in this context that in a letter to the composer, welcoming him to Stockholm in September 1961, he singled out the *Symphony of Psalms* as having had great influence on his own work.)[23] Thus in the Graveyard scene he introduced a silhouette of three Gothic steeples, a detail which apparently met with Stravinsky's approval,[24] evoking the shadow of Calvary and so vesting Tom, already Rake, Orpheus, Faust and Adonis, with the further attributes of Christ.

In the following year, on 2 February 1962, the opera was added to the repertory of Sadler's Wells Opera in a production by Glen Byam Shaw, conducted by Colin Davis, with a cast including Alexander Young as Tom, Elsie Morison as Anne, Raimund Herincx as Shadow and Ann Robson as Baba. This production enjoyed great success in London and on tour abroad, and it drew Stravinsky to London in June 1964 to conduct a second commercial recording of the work, again for Columbia, using the Sadler's Wells chorus. But equally important to this recording was the concert performance at the Metropolitan Opera on 20 November 1962, conducted by Robert Craft and given under the auspices of the American Opera Society. The cast, led by Alexander Young again, Judith Raskin as Anne, John Reardon as Shadow and Betty Allen as Baba, provided Stravinsky with the principals for his disc version, except that Allen was replaced by Regina Sarfaty.

The composer's eighty-fifth birthday, in 1967, was marked by a number of new productions, including those of the Hamburg Staatsoper by Gian-Carlo Menotti, the Berlin Staatsoper by Carl Ebert once more,

12 Sadler's Wells 1962: the Brothel scene, with Alexander Young as Tom

Scottish Opera by his son Peter Ebert (at the Edinburgh Festival, with Alexander Gibson conducting and Alexander Young again as the Rake) and Oxford University Opera Club by Michael Meneaugh. But more curious than any of these was the Boston Opera production by Sarah Caldwell, which was unveiled on 17 March and which brought the action forward to the present. Act I scene 2 was made to take place in a discothèque, and the last act's graveyard was one for motor cars, lit by the headlights of a Rolls-Royce hearse. Craft recorded, however, that the most complete success was the Auction scene:

> Sellem — Hawaiian shirt, hippy beads, gardenia over the ear — is a combination Guru, con man, TV automobile salesman. He sits crosslegged on a Simeon-like stylite hoisted from stage level, and as he reels off the objects under the gavel, photographs of them are flashed on the curtain in the manner of a fast-moving slide lecture. The bidders, who have infiltrated the audience in Café La Mama style, move closer to the orchestra as each lot is sold, until they stand by the pit itself for the balance of promises and a better view of Baba resuscitated on TV.[25]

The year that would have seen Stravinsky's ninetieth birthday, 1972, was again the occasion for many new productions, by the Netherlands Opera, the Deutsche Oper am Rhein, the São Carlos company of Lisbon, the Prague National Theatre (this the first production in Czech), the Teatro Comunale of Florence and other companies. And since then the work has continued to be widely performed: indeed, it must have enjoyed more productions than any other opera composed since the death of Puccini, though few of these have been as witty and successful as two English productions of the 1970s. Glyndebourne presented their second version for the first time on 26 June 1975, conducted by Bernard Haitink, produced by John Cox, designed by David Hockney, and with a cast including Leo Goeke as Tom, Jill Gomez as Anne, Donald Gramm as Shadow and Rosalind Ellis as Baba. Then the opera at last reached Covent Garden, nearly three decades after Webster had been angling for it, on 18 June 1979, the ninety-seventh anniversary of Stravinsky's birth, when it was conducted by Sir Colin Davis, produced by Elijah Moshinsky and designed by Timothy O'Brien and Tazeena Firth, with a cast led by Robert Tear as Tom, Helen Donath as Anne, Donald Gramm again and Patricia Johnson as Baba.

The Glyndebourne production inevitably drew attention most particularly for the Hockney sets and costumes, which were reproduced for the Milan production of 1979 and which were, to be sure, startling yet wholly apt. The idea of going back to Hogarth's manner and groupings had been employed in Bergman's version and many others (few directors have not recognised that the third painting corresponds with

Performance history

Act I scene 2 and the eighth with the final scene), and the use of the gravure motif had been a feature of Caldwell's 1967 production. However, it was left to Hockney to conceive designs in which the potential greyness of close stripes and cross-hatching was wholly avoided, in which instead the effect was of vibrant colour, fresh shades of green, red and blue being used more often than black, and used in clean open networks of lines. So, in employing eighteenth-century conventions towards the creation of a distinctively personal and entirely twentieth-century product, he achieved something relating quite exactly to the opera.[26]

At the same time there were simple and striking inventions in the stage furniture: a huge bed on which Mother Goose could claim her due from Tom, and an awful array of boxes in which the madmen appeared at once as corpses, dread witnesses and toys. In this respect there was a connection with the Covent Garden production, which similarly benefited from telling additions to the stage, not least a balcony on each side, allowing characters to stand aside at junctures and so observe the play in which they must take part. There was thus an atmosphere of charade, heightened by having the Rake adopt the look and demeanour of the young Auden, all slicked-back silver hair, self-confident cynicism and cigarette. There may be no more reason in *The Rake's Progress* than in any other work of fiction to assume an identification between hero and author, but here the introduction of the Auden persona was valuable in opening a fissure between appearance and reality, maker and made, that cracked illuminatingly through this deeply ironic work, for if the Rake is creator of his own Progress, then our sympathy with him cannot be mere pity but must be a recognition of his failings as generally human. And though the period of the action was moved to the mid-nineteenth century — where, as Bryan Magee remarked, 'the material heaviness of wealth, the weight and hypocrisy of public opinion, in fact the whole rags-to-riches-to-destruction story, take on additional point and substance'[27] — the visual world was one that could contain a modern poet in a classical plot, a bit of twentieth-century popular dance routine for two nineteenth-century gentlemen (at the end of Act II scene 1, as they go off to win Baba), and a baroque canvas, Poussin's *Realm of Flora*, as drop curtain. It was a world, like that of Stravinsky's music, of congruent incongruities.

13 Glyndebourne 1975: the Auction scene

14 Covent Garden 1979: the Auction scene

6 *Some thoughts on the libretto*
BY GABRIEL JOSIPOVICI

> *Rakewell*: Return! and Love!
> The banished words torment!

No two works of Stravinsky are alike, but *The Rake's Progress* is more different than most.

As we look back over that amazing list of masterpieces, what strikes us now is the unity of the entire canon. From *The Rite of Spring* to *Abraham and Isaac* half a century later the 'feel' of a Stravinsky work is unmistakable: that combination of a hieratic, ritualistic style with a wonderfully lively and witty texture. (The only comparable achievement is the work of the late Yeats.) This is particularly evident in the stage works. *'Les Noces'*, Stravinsky said, 'presents rather than tells.' Here, as in *Oedipus*, the music and the stage action *show* a ritual unfolding, much as a priest might show an icon to the crowd, in André Boucourechlev's apt analogy. These works eschew expressivity, psychology and mimesis; they do not say 'I am' or 'I wish', but 'It is' and 'It shall be.'

The great exception is *The Rake's Progress*. From 1910 to 1945 Stravinsky had written music that often made use of the past but had extremely little to do with European art since the Renaissance. Like Eliot and Kafka, and unlike Mann and Yeats, he made the break with the nineteenth century almost at the start of his career; like Eliot he forged a radical style out of the fragmentation of the past; like Eliot he renewed a whole language by so doing; and like him he wrote highly complex works which are nevertheless immediately accessible – at a visceral rather than an intellectual level. Yet though Stravinsky knew and admired Eliot, and indeed later set some of his work, it was not to Eliot but to Auden that he turned for the libretto to his opera. Auden, of course, had learnt much from Eliot, but his instinct was very different. Though his subject matter was just as contemporary as Eliot's and his range infinitely wider, his approach to art was more traditional, and deliberately so. He believed that one should use language to *talk about* rather than to *show*; in other words he accepted the human limitations of language and contented himself with making poems that smile at their own inadequacies rather than attempting to break through to some totally new mode of expression.

A good way of describing the difference between *The Rake's Progress* and other Stravinsky works is to say that it stands in the same relation to them as Auden does to Eliot. But why did Stravinsky turn to Auden when he decided that the time had come to write a proper opera, and why did he accept a libretto as far removed as it is possible to get from the sacred joyfulness of *The Wedding* or the hieratic awesomeness of *Oedipus*? Why did he put up with the whimsy of Baba the Turk and the Bread Machine or the triteness of the Epilogue? These are more than rhetorical questions, for we know that Stravinsky was never the kind of composer who gratefully accepts whatever his librettist gives him. On the contrary, one major reason for the success of his theatre pieces is surely that in every case he seemed to know exactly what he wanted from his librettist and made sure he got it. He did not simply ask Cocteau for an adaptation of the Sophoclean tragedy. He knew that he wanted the text to be in Latin, not Greek or French; he knew exactly how he wanted text and narration to relate to each other; he had a very clear idea of the way the work should be staged. And this is as true of *Baize* and *Histoire du Soldat* and *The Wedding* as it is of *Oedipus*. Therefore, unless the war, the move to America and the personal tragedies that beset his life in those years had wrought a total change in him, we must accept the fact that the libretto of *The Rake's Progress* is as it is because that is how the composer wanted it to be. And Stravinsky's own remarks on the collaboration bear this out: he approached Auden with the idea; Auden was enthusiastic and came out to California; in ten days the two of them had mapped out the basic structure; Auden and Kallman then set to work to fill in the detail, and although many fine ideas emerged on the way, the initial shape hardly altered. The truth of the matter is that Auden and Stravinsky were so perfectly in tune with each other – 'I discovered [when we began to work together] that we shared the same views not only about opera, but also on the nature of the Beautiful and the Good. Thus, our opera is indeed, and in the highest sense, a collaboration', Stravinsky remarked later – that the words only serve to deepen and enrich the initial conception. Paradoxically this means that though the librettists perfectly fulfil their humble role of providing a scaffold for the music, this is one of the few librettos that can be read and enjoyed on its own.

But we have not yet answered the question of why it was that Stravinsky chose this librettist and this form. The answer will only fully emerge when we have examined the libretto in some detail, but it should perhaps be provisionally sketched in here. Each new work of Stravinsky's, like each new work of Eliot's or Picasso's, was a new departure, a unique solution to a problem most of their contemporaries had not even envisaged. None of them was content ever to repeat himself, and from the start none of them was content to repeat or even merely extend the work of the nineteenth-century masters. Though it is possible now to see connections with Tchaikovsky, Browning or Cézanne, in the end these are far less important than the sense we get from their work of the complete abandonment of a Renaissance Humanist tradition for a more primitive and impersonal art. But the abandoned tradition, the tradition of the classical style, of the novel and narrative poem, of imitation and perspective, is not quite a tradition like any other. It is the result of an effort to see man in a human time and space; it presents man not as he is in an absolute way but as he knows and thinks himself to be in the ordinary course of his life. *The Wedding* and *Oedipus*, like *Prufrock* and *The Waste Land*, are not about the ordinary moments of life. They are, it is true, about ordinary men and women — you, *hypocrite lecteur* — but at extreme moments, when we are taken up into the dance of the universe, when the reality we cannot bear very much of is forced upon us. The polemical nature of these works is evident. They are criticisms of Verdian opera, Browning monologues, Dickensian novels. Man, as he is presented in those forms, is like a person shut up in a railway carriage with all the blinds down. He lives out his life in the carriage, unaware that the train is hurtling forward in a manner totally out of his own control. What *The Waste Land* and *Oedipus* do is to lift the blinds for an instant and show us the truth.

But what of those other times, the normal times celebrated by the nineteenth-century forms? Is the only comment, 'Ridiculous the waste sad time before and after'? *The Rake's Progress* is Stravinsky's attempt to explore those areas of human experience out of which the rest of his music tries to draw us, those areas where man is caught up neither in the primitive dance nor in the sacred procession. More than that: it is about the *relation* of ordinary life to those central moments; about the way in which man, in the normal course of events, turns away from the dance and in so doing denies both reality and himself.

The Wedding and *Oedipus* exist in a timeless world. The celebration of a wedding is an event that takes place outside time; in *Oedipus* the clocks are stopped and for the hero start to run backwards. That is one reason why we feel that these works belong outside our Renaissance and Humanist traditions. For time, the ticking of the clock, is the obsessive post-Renaissance theme, finding expression in the legends of Dr Faustus and Don Juan. By the nineteenth-century — the century of

Some thoughts on the libretto

Progress, as it is often called – the obsession with time is no longer something to be objectified and expressed; it inheres in the very fabric of society and in the very forms of art. Reading the great novels of the era or listening to Berlioz or Verdi we are bound to recall that this was the great period of the railway: the strong momentum drives one forward; once the plot starts to unfold there is no turning to right or left or ever going back. It is interesting to note that in an eighteenth-century novel the chapters tend to be self-contained units, separate panels; whereas by the mid-nineteenth century they are merely convenient divisions in a swelling narrative. What seems to happen in Wagner is that both the heroes and the music itself start to become aware of the horror of this headlong forward rush, but this awareness only serves to reinforce the sense of the protagonists being caught in a seamless web of continuity. Both heroes and music, in Wagner as in Berg, struggle to free themselves from the web, to deny time and its workings, but it is a struggle which can only end in the destruction of the self: the only way to deny time is to die. Hence our sense that the music itself passionately longs for its own annihilation.

This is where Stravinsky's *formal* solution to the problem of writing an opera is so interesting: rather than seek musical forms 'symbolically expressive of the dramatic content (as in the Daedalian examples of Alban Berg)', he has said,

I chose to cast *The Rake* in the mould of an eighteenth-century 'number' opera, one in which the dramatic progress depends on the succession of separate pieces – recitatives and arias, duets, trios, choruses, instrumental interludes. In the earlier scenes the mould is to some extent pre-Gluck in that it tends to crowd the story into the secco recitatives, reserving the arias for the reflective poetry, but then, as the opera warms up, the story is told, enacted, contained almost entirely in song – as distinguished from so-called speech-song, and Wagnerian continuous melody, which consists, in effect, of orchestral commentary enveloping continuous recitative.

Curiously, what happens here is that an opera which denies the unfolding of time in its form is able to *examine* time and its workings in a way which an opera that lives under the aegis of time (like *Tristan* or *Wozzeck*) never can. *The Rake's Progress* does not ignore the problem of time by devising a form that by-passes the issue, as does *Oedipus*. It had to be Auden and not Eliot who would provide the libretto to Stravinsky's only full-length opera because in that work Stravinsky wanted to explore the problem of the relation between music and narrative, which is the relation between the ideal timeless world of the imagination and the everyday human world of time and death and such human and social things as promises and wishes. *The Rake's Progress* is thus at once a comment on life and on the genre — opera — in which it chooses to exist.

The Wedding had celebrated marriage as a rite and a sacrament; *The Rake's Progress* charts the consequences of refusing to take part in a sacramental union. The opera opens, like many a Shakespearian comedy, with the praise of a Golden Age:

> *Anne*: The woods are green and bird and beast at play
> For all things keep this festival of May;
> With fragrant odours and with notes of cheer
> The pious earth observes the solemn year.
> *Rakewell*: Now is the season when the Cyprian Queen
> With genial charm translates our mortal scene,
> When swains their nymphs in fervent arms enfold
> And with a kiss restore the Age of Gold.

Music, which, as Auden says, 'is for everyone and no-one, and is always in the Present Tense', is ideally suited to celebrate the restoration of the Age of Gold. This is the Paradise of the Imagination, when all our wishes are fulfilled. But though it is real insofar as we can imagine it, it is false insofar as it ignores the reality of space and time in which we live. Opera is, ideally, a wedding of music and words; that is, of imagination and reality. But such a union is impossible, as the greatest operas have always recognised. Monteverdi's *Orfeo*, with which *The Rake's Progress* has much in common, also starts with the celebration of a joyful union which brings with it echoes of a Golden Age, but its central theme is the lament for the loss of that union. In *Don Giovanni* the central issue is the irreconcilable conflict between the immediacy of music, embodied in Don Giovanni himself, and the claims of society and of ethics.

In a Shakespearian comedy the ideal of the opening is usually shattered by a father figure who insists on his rights by law to destroy the frail paradise of the lovers. Such comedy usually ends with the father recognising the primacy of Nature over Law and giving his blessing to the lovers. The Maytime of the opening thus returns, reinforced by the trials to which it has been subjected. *The Rake's Progress* begins its re-evaluation of post-Renaissance assumptions by subverting this basic form. For Trulove, Anne's father, is, as his name implies, not a tyrannical father but one who, unlike Rakewell, loves truly:

Trulove: Tom, I have news for you. I have spoken on your behalf to a good friend in the City, and he offers you a position in his countinghouse.
Rakewell: You are too generous, sir. You must not think me ungrateful if I do not immediately accept what you propose, but I have other prospects in view.

Trulove: Your reluctance to seek steady employment makes me uneasy.
Rakewell: Be assured your daughter shall not marry a poor man.
Trulove: So he be honest, she may take a poor husband if she choose, but I am resolved she shall never marry a lazy one.

Rakewell's comment on this is: 'The old fool!', but Trulove is no fool, though he may be a bore. He is asking Tom to recognise that by marrying he is entering a world of responsibility, which means a world where Time and Money have to be recognised and accepted. For time and love go hand in hand, since love implies commitment in time to another person; and in our world if two people are to live together at least one of them will have to give a thought to money. In *Tristan* music and time are deeply at odds, and music finally triumphs over time in a death which is also erotic fulfilment. *The Rake*, on the other hand, is committed from the first to the musical articulation of the acceptance of time. Time is not denied by the action, but the consequences of such a denial *by the hero* are examined and commented upon, so that the opera is able to explore the relation of human beings to time in a way *Tristan* never can.

Tom's response to his future father-in-law is 'I will trust Fortune.' This sounds very much like the remark of one of Shakespeare's clowns, and our sympathies, it would seem, should go with him and against the bourgeois ethics of Trulove. But the central fact about the Shakespearian clown is that he is alone, whereas Tom has committed himself in the opening duet to Anne. By this act – singing his love with the other person is a public act equivalent in opera to taking an oath in church in real life – he has entered the world of responsibility, and therefore of time and money, whether he likes it or not. And indeed his next remark is 'I wish I had money', a sentiment no Shakespearian clown would ever express. It is quite natural too that the expression of the wish should bring Shadow onto the stage. Though 'many insist' that he 'does not exist', yet his task is to carry out such wishes and then extort the price. In the opera he appears as the parody of a Dickensian *deus ex machina*, with his talk of rich uncles and advantageous wills, and proceeds to whisk Tom off to London.

The first scene is a sort of prelude, since it ends with Shadow addressing the audience with the words: 'The Progress of a Rake begins.' It hovers between the ideal world of Renaissance mythologising and the practical world of bourgeois capitalist enterprise. The second scene sets the opera firmly in the eighteenth century – or rather in the late eighteenth century, for this is not the poised and polished world of the Augustans but the nervous and anguished world of Dr Johnson and Diderot, of Hogarth and Sade; a world which has lost faith in the ground of eighteenth-century beliefs but has not yet found a vocabulary to express this, and where there is consequently a tension between the heavy impersonal style and diction and the sense of desperate uncertainty beneath. This tension comes out clearly in the catechism in the brothel:

>   *Rakewell*: One aim in all things to pursue:
>   My duty to myself to do . . .
>   To shut my eyes to prude and preacher
>   And follow Nature as my teacher . . .
> *Mother Goose*: What is the secret Nature knows?
>   *Rakewell*: What Beauty is and where it grows.
>   *Shadow*: Canst thou define the Beautiful?
>   *Rakewell*: I can.
>   That source of pleasure to the eyes
>   Youth owns, with snatches, money *buys*,
>   Envy affects to scorn, but lies:
>   One fatal flaw it has. It dies.

Mortality, indeed, hangs heavy over this scene. Shadow can turn the clock back but he cannot annihilate Time. The philosophy, as in Sade, is one of despair; Love's triumphant campaigns are not at all a fulfilling of nature, for the view of Nature expressed here leaves out an essential element in human nature — and the despair stems from the fact that it half senses that it does so:

> Soon dawn will glitter outside the shutter
> And small birds twitter, but what of that?
> So long as we're able and wine's on the table,
> Who cares what the troubling day is at?
>
> While food has flavour and limbs are shapely
> And hearts beat bravely to fiddle or drum
> Our proper employment is reckless enjoyment
> For too soon the noiseless night will come.

Dreams are only dreams, the imagination only imagination; man can glut his senses as much as he wishes but he will not be able to shut out the thoughts of his own mortality. Where Wagner tried through sheer will-power to force reality to conform to desire, Auden and Stravinsky begin with an acceptance of the way things are:

> Sweet dreams, my master. Dreams may lie,
> But dream. For when you wake, you die.

This is why that second scene is so suffused with sadness, a sadness lifted to a strange height in the wonderful setting of 'The sun is bright, the grass is green; Lanterloo, lanterloo', which Stravinsky called 'the most wonderful gift a librettist ever made to a composer', but which is also one of the most wonderful repayments ever made by a composer to his librettist. By giving this supremely innocent music to the roaring boys and whores the composer retrospectively calls into question the opening duet. As Golding says, there is no innocent work. To portray innocence is to destroy it. That is why pastoral is such a disturbing genre. Conversely, by portraying the loss of innocence we may be led to a rediscovery of it, on the other side of despair, as Tom will do. In *Tristan* and *Wozzeck* it is music that dies at the end, as the hero dies, finally engulfed by the world of reality. In *The Rake* the ultimate renunciation happens at the very start, with the composer's own renunciation of expressivity ('rather than seek musical forms symbolically expressive of the dramatic content . . .'). He accepts that there is no innocent work, that music cannot by itself portray innocence or guilt, that it cannot finally convey the feelings of either the characters or the composer (that is why he says the opera is so bound up with *Cosi fan tutte*). Schoenberg, faced with such a realisation, took the drastic step of having his hero refuse to sing; as always Stravinsky's solution is at once more and less radical — less radical because all the characters go on singing away merrily; more radical because his solution involves a rethinking of the form, not merely the content, of opera.

By siding with Shadow rather than Trulove, Tom has denied Time, Love, and, ultimately, his own nature. Each of his three wishes draws him further along the road of denial and despair. Since the two latter wishes — 'I wish I were happy' and 'I wish it were true' — lead to the two most whimsical and arbitrary episodes in the opera — the episodes of Baba and of the Bread Machine — it is worth pausing over them for a moment.

Both Baba and the Bread Machine look at first as though they would fill the gap left by the denial of Anne/Love. Both prove illusory. Between them, however, these two improbable episodes span the major obsessions of the nineteenth century, the century of Freedom and Progress. In the first scene of Act II Shadow explains to Tom why he is suggesting a marriage between him and Baba:

Come, master, observe the host of mankind. How are they? Wretched. Why? Because they are not free. Why? Because the giddy multitude are driven by the unpredictable Must of their pleasures and the sober few are bound by the inflexible Ought of their duty, between which slaveries there is nothing to choose. Would you be happy? Then learn to act freely. Would you act freely? Then learn to ignore those twin tyrants of appetite and conscience. Therefore I counsel you, master — take Baba the Turk to wife.

But the *acte gratuit* can never bring real freedom, for there the will acts in a void. Freedom implies responsibility, the acknowledgement that one is bound by one's choices. The argument is not between morality and freedom, as Tom, like Sade, keeps trying to make it. Nor is it, in musical terms, a conflict between the imposition of order and the indulgence of sensations. It is precisely this sense of responsibility that distinguishes the major from the minor artist in any age.

Tom's third wish is prompted by his dream of the machine that can turn stones to bread. When Shadow shows him the machine of his dreams he immediately imagines that to present this to the world will solve all its problems and will thus be the good deed that can make him deserve Anne's love again. For:

> Thanks to this excellent device
> Man shall re-enter Paradise
>   From which he once was driven.
> Secure from need, the cause of crime,
> The world shall for the second time
>   Be similar to Heaven.

After the Utopia of Freedom, the Utopia of Progress. But the audience has seen Shadow put the bread in the machine in the first place, and thus knows that the 'engine' is a fraud. The effect of this bit of stage-play is difficult to analyse, but I would suggest that what we see in the machine is an analogue of the opera itself, the 'machine' made by Auden and Stravinsky.

The mechanical nature of Stravinsky's music has often been noted. He himself tells us that his problem with *The Wedding* was to find an orchestration that 'would be at the same time perfectly homogeneous, perfectly impersonal, and perfectly mechanical'. This quality is of course the one we tend to associate with the hieratic and ritualistic, the one that makes us feel the works 'show' rather than express or describe. But part of the effect comes from an acceptance by the music of itself as only music, the product of sounds made by specific instruments, rather than as a great river carrying the listener off into another world. This music is made, rather than simply existing like a force of nature; it belongs to the Secondary, rather than the Primary world. In one sense it is no better than the Bread Machine, since it is an 'engine' and a purely man-made and unmiraculous one at that. The paradox here of course is that the insistence on its Secondary nature allows such art to transcend the mechanical; whereas an art which imagines that it is reaching out into the unknown all too often strikes us as expressive only of the composer's own banal obsessions.

The Romantics and the Liberal-Progressives of the nineteenth century were at one in refusing to accept man's fallen nature. They thus railed at society and at man himself for the position in which he found himself. The most profound thinkers of the century – Kierkegaard, Dostoevsky, Nietzsche – realised that it is necessary to start from the premise of man's fallen condition, of the impossibility of innocence. Only in this way could there be any realistic appraisal of man's nature. In recognising this they were of course only touching again on a religious tradition whose greatest exemplars are St Augustine and Dante, and it is to this tradition that both Stravinsky and Auden felt themselves emphatically to belong. In the present age, however, it seems probable that such a tradition can only find its voice through the negation of its opposite. The problem is highlighted in the creation of the figure of Anne in the opera.

Anne's first words after Tom's departure for London set before us the artistic as well as the psychological problem:

> No word from Tom. Has Love no voice, can Love not keep
> A Maytime vow in winter? . . .
> He needs my help. Love hears. Love knows . . .
> If love be love
> It will not alter . . .

She can only be a presence, as love itself can only be felt as a force, not expressed in words.

Her next appearance, however, in the fifth and central scene of the opera, makes the dilemma most manifest. She has at last found Tom in London, only to discover that he is married to Baba. As he steps out of his chair he recognises her in the gloom outside his house. He reacts guiltily and violently:

> *Rakewell*: Anne, ask me, accuse me –
> *Anne*: Tom, no –
> *Rakewell*: – Denounce me to the world, and go;
> Return to your home, forget in your senses
> What, senseless, you pursue.

At once Anne picks up his word: 'Do you return?' He is shaken: 'I?' She persists: 'Then how shall I go?'

> *Rakewell*: You must!
> (*aside*) O wilful powers, pummel to dust
> And drive into the void, one thought – return!

The one thought he cannot face is that conjured up by the word *return*. Anne is not of course simply talking about a physical return to her father's house and the country. She is asking him to return *to* her as well as *with* her. But this is the one thing Tom cannot do. For, in his denial of time, he is driven on in a frenzied progress *by* time. Only through his acceptance of time, which would mean his acceptance of the validity of his vow to Anne, could he find a release from time, and with that the possibility of return.

In his notes to *New Year Letter*, glossing the line 'Hell is the being of the lie', Auden makes the following comment, which has a direct bearing on Tom's position. 'It is possible', he writes,

> that the gates of Hell are always standing wide open. The lost are perfectly free to leave whenever they like, but to do so would mean admitting that the gates were open, that is, that there was another life outside. This they cannot admit, not because they have any pleasure in their present existence, but because the life outside would be different, and, if they admitted its existence, they would have to lead it. They know this. They know that they are free to leave and they know why they do not. This knowledge is the flame of Hell.

In Dante the damned in Hell cling to their identities in defiance of God, willing themselves into being and refusing to accept anything outside their own egos. In the upper reaches of Hell they go endlessly round and round the same circle, to which they have been condemned by eternal decree; in the lower reaches they grow more and more fixed to a single spot, until near the very centre they are frozen in the ice and even their tears cannot flow. In Purgatory the pilgrims are free of this; they wind round and round the mountain cone, moving ever upwards towards the Earthly Paradise. The word *tornare* occurs often in that canticle, as fitting where the theme is the celebration of those who were supple enough to turn to God in repentance before their death. In Eliot's most Dantean poem, *Ash Wednesday,* the starting point is Cavalcanti's famous lament on his own exile: 'Perch' i' no spero di tornar giammai', which Eliot at first renders as 'Because I do not hope to turn again'. But the form of the poem is itself a slow, hesitant gradual spiralling, and the poem (in contrast to the fragmentation of *The Waste Land* and the other early poems) moves forwards and upwards, until in the last section the opening lines are transformed into:

> Although I do not hope to turn again
> Although I do not hope
> Although I do not hope to turn . . .

Stravinsky never changes his style in so radical a fashion. Yet *The Rake's Progress* becomes the place where the exploration of the meaning of turn and return — in psychological and aesthetic terms — is most protracted. To follow it through we now need to move on to the last two scenes.

A year has passed. Shadow, in the graveyard, claims his wages: Rake-

Some thoughts on the libretto

well's soul. Rakewell is terrified, and the clock starts to strike the fatal hour. However, Shadow stops it short and agrees to play a game: for Tom's three wishes, three cards; if he guesses what they are, he is free; if not, he belongs to Shadow.

The first card is picked. Tom, thinking suddenly and unexpectedly of Anne and of her love for him, makes a desperate guess: the Queen of Hearts. The guess is correct. The second card is picked. As Tom struggles to guess, a spade falls beside them, and Tom curses: 'The deuce!' He looks round, sees the cause of the noise, and says calmly:

> She lights the shades
> And shows -- the two of spades.

Shadow acknowledges his good luck:

> The two of spades.
> Congratulations. The Goddess still is faithful.

Now comes the final card. Shadow is ironic: 'Think on your hopes.' 'O God', answers Tom in despair, 'what hopes have I?' As he turns away Shadow picks up the discarded Queen of Hearts and replaces it in the pack. He addresses the audience:

> The simpler the trick, the simpler the deceit;
> That there is no return, I've taught him well,
>   And repetition palls him:
> The Queen of Hearts shall be for him the Queen of Hell.

By offering Tom the Queen of Hearts again he wishes not simply to trick him, but in so doing to confirm Tom in his servitude to him and to Time, and, by making him deny Anne once and for all, to deny any possibility of redemption.

Tom, knowing his hour has come at last, looks away from the spot and sees: 'Dear God, a track of cloven hooves'. Shadow is scornful:

> The knavish goats are back
> To crop the spring's return.

He knows Tom will not believe him, will not even imagine that he wishes to be believed. It is obvious that the tracks are made by his own cloven hooves, denying the return of any spring for Tom — that spring celebrated so joyfully at the start of the opera. But Tom pounces on Shadow's word as Anne had pounced on his:

> *Rakewell*: Return! and Love!
>   The banished words torment.
> *Shadow*: You cannot now repent.

The word Shadow has spoken has a life of its own — none of our words are exclusively ours, we can never know what echoes they will awake in another mind and heart. This is in part the burden of responsibility in the human use of language: our words only gain meaning and coherence by the meaning and coherence of the lives and thoughts of those who speak them. So now, suddenly, unexpectedly, Tom moves out of Shadow's clutches and into a wholly new world. Out of his mouth come the words: 'Return O Love – ', and at that moment the miracle happens and the voice of Anne does indeed return, singing:

> A love
> That is sworn before Thee can plunder hell
> of its prey.

Tom listens, spellbound, and then says simply:

> I wish for nothing else.
> Love, first and last, assume eternal reign;
> Renew my life, O Queen of Hearts again.

And with Tom's acceptance of return and renewal, Shadow vanishes.

But this is not a fairy story. Love can plunder Hell and rob it of its prey, the spirit even of a rake is supple enough to repent at last and turn and return if his lover's love is steadfast. But there is a price to pay. Having betrayed love as he has, he can only find it again, and fulfilled, in madness, just as in *Orfeo* it is only in Heaven that Orfeo and Eurydice can be perpetually united once Orfeo has looked back. In this last scene of the opera the echoes of *Orfeo* grow strong again. Tom, who in the opening duet had invoked the figures of Venus and Adonis, now, in Bedlam, believes that he is Adonis and will answer to no other name. Nevertheless, he is lucid about his own errors, and though greeting Anne as 'Venus' when she comes to visit him, tells her:

> In a foolish dream, in a gloomy labyrinth
> I hunted shadows, disdaining thy true love;
> Forgive thy servant, who repents his madness,
> Forgive Adonis and he shall faithful prove.

But Anne answers:

> What should I forgive? Thy ravishing penitence
> Blesses me, dear heart, and brightens all the past.
> Kiss me Adonis: the wild boar is vanquished.
> *Rakewell*: Embrace me, Venus; I've come home at last.
> *Rakewell and Anne*: Rejoice, beloved: in these fields of Elysium
> Space cannot alter, nor Time our love abate;
> Here has no words for absence or estrangement
> Nor Now a notion of Almost or Too Late.

But reality has words for 'Almost' and 'Too Late', and though music celebrates the present, in this opera the present attains its poignancy because it is so clearly situated between a past and a future. Just as Orfeo and Eurydice are united only in Heaven, so Tom can become Adonis and shed his earthly self to unite with Venus/Anne only in a madhouse. And since madness, unlike love, cannot be shared, she has eventually to leave him. Here, at the end of the opera, words and music combine to express in miraculous fashion the simultaneous presence of loss and gain, of the fulfilment of desire and its inevitable frustration:

Rakewell: Where art thou, Venus? Venus, where art thou? The flowers, open to the sun. The birds renew their song. It is spring. The bridal couch is prepared. Come quickly, beloved, and we will celebrate the holy rites of love. Holla! Achilles, Helen, Eurydice, Orpheus, Persephone, Plato, all my courtiers. Holla!
Where is my Venus? Why have you stolen her while I slept? Madmen! Where have you hidden her? . . . My heart breaks. I feel the chill of death's approaching wing. Orpheus, strike from thy lyre a swan-like music, and weep, ye nymphs and shepherds of these Stygian fields, weep for Adonis the beautiful, the young; weep for Adonis whom Venus loved.

The image of Venus and Adonis, which was purely rhetorical and conventional in the opening duet, is now fully placed and accepted. Such an eternal union can be conceived by the human imagination, but it can be achieved only in the timeless world of the stars. On earth our art can only give such longing a body, and a responsible art must lament its impossibility. Thus is Romantic longing expressed and put in perspective in some of Stravinsky's most human and haunting music.

The mood of that music is immediately shattered by the sprightly Epilogue. But that too is essential to the overall pattern. Had we been left with the action and music of the ninth scene we would have been tempted to enter fully into Tom's mind. and to accept the world of his madness as in some sense the real world. (This is what Maxwell Davies, whose temperament is more akin to a Romantic like Schoenberg than to Stravinsky, does at the end of his *Songs for a Mad King*, when he turns the impersonal spoken lament into the King's howl of anguish and leaves us with that ringing in our ears.) It is right for this opera that the frame should be deliberately replaced at the end, that we should return from the heavens, from the music of longing and lament, to the light and society music of the eighteenth century. What we have seen and heard, after all, the Epilogue reminds us, is only a cunning engine devised by Auden and Stravinsky, ordinary mortals if extraordinary artists. There is no absolute gulf between them and ourselves, only differing degrees of clarity and skill.

I have tried to show how well the libretto of *The Rake's Progress* suits the composer's purpose, and to define a little more precisely what that purpose might have been. I have also wanted to show that this seemingly whimsical and sometimes frivolous work stands as a critique, and not just an alternative, to the 'continuous' opera of Wagner and Berg. That this form corresponded not just to a conscious decision on Stravinsky's part but also to an instinctive mode of composing is hardly surprising. The great artist is the one who is able to objectify his obsessions and, by finding appropriate forms for them, to purge both himself and us. In his diary for 1951 Robert Craft notes that Stravinsky, at about the time of the première of *The Rake's Progress*, remarked that his brothers used to call him 'the piano tuner' because of his obsessions with and constant repetition of notes that he liked. Such a need to go back to the same note or group of notes again and again is characteristic of his music from the start. *The Rake's Progress*, seen in the light of that remark, is perhaps the one work of Stravinsky's which gives a justification in terms of human psychology, and of the realities of our world, for that obsessional need to repeat and return. It is the piano tuner's answer to the train driver.

7 In an operatic graveyard: Act III scene 2

The very specialness of the Graveyard scene in the third act will already be obvious from a reading of the synopsis above (pp. 31 – 47). It is the climax of the drama, the scene in which the Rake progresses furthest in self-knowledge: he comes to understand the nature of his Shadow and of his real wants, and with the destruction of his partial self he loses his wits. Moreover, it is the only scene in the whole opera to feature just the two principal characters, just as its immediate predecessor, the Auction scene, is the only one in which they do not appear, apart from Anne's short solo scene at the end of Act I.

Their absence from the Auction scene – the absence, therefore, of any dominating figure – is the opportunity for Stravinsky and his librettists to create here the only image of a society in the opera. Wherever the chorus has appeared before, in the Brothel scene and in the scene of Baba's homecoming, it has been as a unified mass, divided at the most into groups of men and of women, and it will be the same again in the Bedlam scene at the end of the work. In these scenes, too, Stravinsky's almost exclusively chordal treatment of the choral voices, following his practice in *The Wedding* and the sacred pieces of the thirties and forties, emphasises the oneness of the crowd, while the text similarly gives it only generalised sentiments. By contrast, in the Auction scene the chorus becomes a collection of individuals. The writing is still largely in declaimed chords, and what the chorus says is still the murmur of the mob, but now it is involved throughout in the action of the scene, and in the bidding episodes a few separate voices are allowed to emerge.

Another peculiarity of the Auction scene is that its main character is Sellem, who does not appear anywhere else in the opera, not even in the Epilogue, despite the fact that he has a more conspicuous role than Trulove, who does come forward at the end. Dramatically, therefore, the Auction scene stands out from the rest, and it does so musically as well. Unlike all the other scenes, it ends with the same music that began it, so that within the structure of the work it is framed off – and the framing music is in the key of the opening Prelude, E major, encouraging one to view the scene as an opera within the opera.

And one might suppose further that while this divertissement is in progress the 'real' opera is going on elsewhere, where Tom and Shadow are, off stage. Their interruptions tell us that after the fiasco of the stones-to-bread machine they have no place in normal society, but we hear also how closely master and servant are joined now as one: their ballad couplets declare their indifference to the natural order ('If boys had wings . . . I should not laugh or cry') and to society ('Who cares a fig for Tory or Whig?'), while their music locks them together as an outlaw pair. Even in the authorship of their words Tom and Shadow are apart from the rest, since, as has been noted above (p. 14), their lines are Auden interpolations in a Kallman scene.

Except in this regard, the Graveyard scene turns its predecessor inside out. Tom and Shadow are now on stage alone throughout – again a unique situation – and the music of their first duet grows in part out of the ballad tune, as also does Tom's song at the end. However, the very first page of the scene, the prelude for string quartet, has no connection with the ballad tune or indeed with anything else that has gone before. Even the presence of a prelude is unusual, for this is the only scene apart from the first to have one, and it seems to suggest that the opera is starting up again after the self-contained excursion of the Auction scene. The character of the music, with cello and viola playing softly in a slow tempo for the first eight bars (see Example 1) is in complete contrast

Ex. 1

In an operatic graveyard: Act III scene 2

with what has gone before. Bright, decisive E major is suddenly followed by a troubled and hazy suggestion of B flat minor, full orchestra in loud bustle by two instruments edging quietly along. This again is something strange after Stravinsky's practice in the previous acts, where scenes have been linked by close relations of tonality and no great discord of texture.

More distantly, the quartet prelude is opposed in scoring and manner to the predominantly brass Prelude at the beginning of the opera, and in its tempo it stands out from the great bulk of what has passed hitherto. *The Rake's Progress* is generally an allegro opera; here for the first time we have a substantial passage of slow music, after which slowness is to be as much the norm as briskness was before. The marked tempo, crotchet = 69, was first used in the opera by Shadow in his quasi-aria 'Fair lady, gracious gentlemen', his first measured number (and this is not an idle observation in a work where tempo is as carefully controlled as key). In this prelude, however, the 3/2 metre and crotchet movement give a very much slower feeling than had the 3/4 and busy semiquavers of the earlier number.

Finally, the prelude to the Graveyard scene has a special place in being the first section of the opera Stravinsky wrote, which makes its sluggish, dark, slipping harmony all the more curious, in that there was no immediate precedent among his works for something so far from tonality. It is as if, in going straight to the crux of the opera, he was jumping right over it and entering prematurely his late period (though the prelude would not appear to enter the serial waters tentatively tested in *Orpheus*). That his first thoughts for the opera should have come in string quartet terms, however, is not so very surprising: he may have been thinking of the example of the sextet for strings at the start of Strauss's then recent *Capriccio* (1940–1), a chamber prelude which similarly ends in F major, or of certain instrumental works by Mozart and Verdi that can readily be linked to their operas. Here the voiceless commentary was coming first.

It continues as tonally ambivalent as it had begun, and from the point where the two violins enter, in the ninth bar, the harmony changes almost on every crotchet, with a crab-like movement in small steps, a sense of confinement enhanced by the restricted spans of the instruments. The final exit into the tonal light of F major is foreseeable only from a short distance, but its establishment is enough to make one look for B flat major in the duet which follows directly. However, this is only one possibility suggested by the typically rootless music that begins the duet. The key might as well be D minor or possibly G minor, and it is

78   The Rake's Progress

only when Tom starts to sing that the bass proclaims the latter, though he still hankers, as so often, after the dominant (see Example 2).

The strengthening of the dominant is of course a common feature of Stravinsky's music of the twenties, thirties and forties, and indeed of neoclassical music in general. In opera it proves a versatile technique.

Ex. 2

In an operatic graveyard: Act III scene 2

It can be used to convey, at one extreme, the overbearing confidence of the roaring boys in the chorus at the start of the Brothel scene, or, at the other, the anxiety and lack of certainty that Tom feels here: the effect depends on whether the vocal music crowns the bass, affirming its own validity, or wavers above in doubt.

Tom's sense of a malign, unsettling strangeness is further presented by rhythmic means. In the ten bars of his first stanza of the duet he sings on the first beat only thrice and on the strong third beat only five times; the 4/8 metre is trickily confounded, as it had been also in the aria 'Vary the song', where again Tom was dissociated from his environment. But it is also worth noting how, though far from usual, Stravinsky's word setting is extraordinarily responsive to accent, quantity and meaning. The iamb 'How dark' is 'correctly' set twice as a lightly accented short note followed by a longer, stronger one, but then in order to help overcome his unwillingness to proceed Tom produces a 'false' heavy accent, as of one steeling himself to a task, hitting for the first time the first beat of the bar, and then hiccoughing onto the word 'dark'. In the following bar the first syllable of 'dreadful' is stressed, as it should be, but Tom hurries over it, not wanting really to acknowledge what he is saying, and in the next bar the weakness of his demand is indicated by the fact that though the 'Why' is a major third above any other note heard so far in the scene, and though it is marked off by large intervals not otherwise found in Tom's line here, it is off the beat, so that the emphasis granted by the pitch factors becomes uncontrolled, almost hysterical.

These are just a few examples, taken from a short section of the opera, but they should give one pause before accepting the common view that the unnaturalness in Stravinsky's word setting was due simply to the fact that he was unfamiliar with the English language. Auden, who might have been expected to object to any incompetent distortion of his text, in fact approved. He recalled:

> Going through our text Stravinsky asked for, and marked into his copy, the spoken rhythmical value of every word. In one instance, only one, did he make a mistake. He thought that in the word 'sedan-chair', the accent fell on the first syllable of 'sedan'. When we pointed this out to him, he immediately altered his score. In one number in the opera, the Auctioneer's aria in Act III, Scene 1, it is dramatically essential that the sung rhythms conform pretty closely to the spoken. They do. In the rest of the work, whatever occasional liberties he took, none of them struck our English and literary ears as impermissible.[1]

Certainly the question does not arise in the case of Shadow's reply, the next segment of the Graveyard duet. Untroubled 3/8 is exchanged for the much confused 4/8, G major for the earlier G minor, pizzicato and light harmonics for the anguished stumbling of the string ensemble, a tempo precisely twice as fast for Tom's slow andante (see Example 3).

Ex. 3

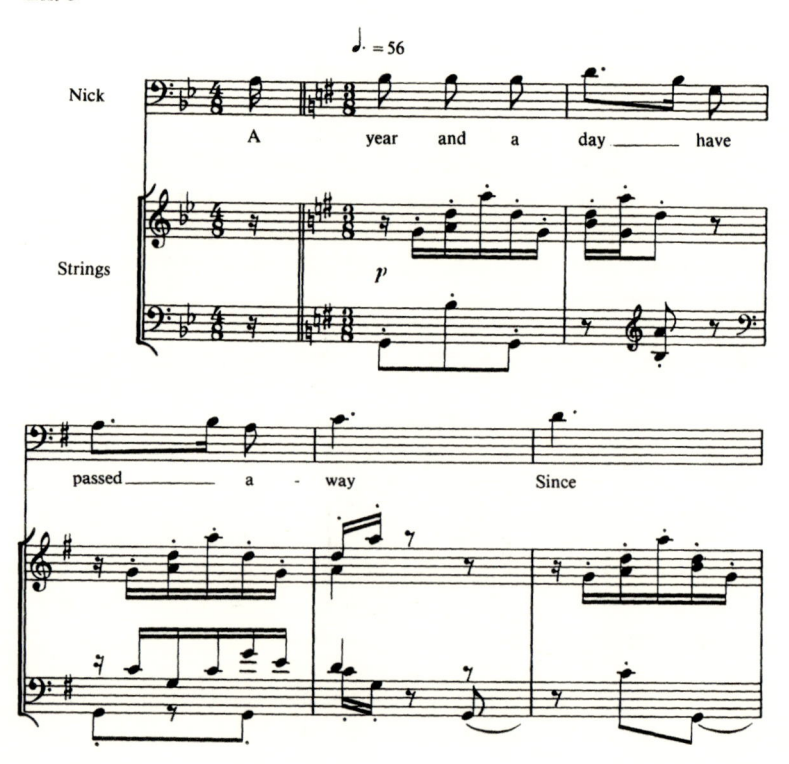

In an operatic graveyard: Act III scene 2

first___ to you I came.

The only thing that stays the same is the ballad metre of the verse, which is indeed a constant throughout this long and complex number — an unusual stability in a libretto that prides itself on variety of movement. The ballad metre, with its implications of vulgar moralising, has belonged to Shadow since his aria 'In youth the panting slave pursues' in Act II scene 1; in the Auction scene its acceptance by Tom underlines how much he has cast himself with Shadow. But now, in the graveyard, he seems to be fighting against the metre while Shadow accepts it without question, and accepts too the ballad tune of the previous scene in all its essentials, though with a drop in key by a minor third.

The urgency in Shadow's stanza, due to the speed and the musical metre, is joined by a feeling of hollowness caused by the offbeat viola and cello harmonics, these replacing the more dependable wind instruments of the ballad tune in the Auction scene. There is no doubt from this that Shadow's business is grim, and he seems in a hurry to get on with it. He blithely ignores Tom's waverings, together with their pace and their key, providing an instance of how the unprepared juxtaposition of musical blocks, which is such a common feature in Stravinsky's music of all periods, can be used to present irreconcilable states of mind.

Indeed, the whole duet is composed from sections that are opposed to one another in tonality and tempo, though all are geared to the same basic speed. The structure is as follows:

A Tom voices his fears   G minor, quaver = 84
B Shadow claims his wages   G major, dotted crotchet = 56 (i.e. twice the tempo of A)
A Tom asks him to be patient   G minor, quaver = 84
B Shadow insists he must have Tom's soul . . .   G major, dotted crotchet = 56

C ... and tells him he must choose the manner of his death	B minor, quaver = 84
D Tom laments his fate; Shadow says it cannot be avoided	G minor to A minor, dotted crotchet = 84 (i.e. three times the tempo of A)
C Shadow repeats his demand	B minor, quaver = 84

Shadow's haste is nicely brought out in his second stanza, where in his hurry to get out the words "Tis not your money but your soul' he forgets his tune, which is carried at the same time by oboe and trumpet. But otherwise the repetitions in the scheme are unmistakable and the contrasts bald, with disjunctions of tempo and key in the later part of the duet that draw attention, as before, to incompatibilities of character. The agitation of the 'D' section – the only passage in the number where both voices are heard at once – is due not only to the metronomic speed but also to the race of semiquavers in the accompaniment under the arching longer notes of the voices, and to the troubled rise in tonality through unstable lurches from G minor by way of A flat minor to A minor. It is also noteworthy that this one moment where the voices are together is not a moment of real communication, for Tom in his fears and Shadow in his gloating are each of them addressing only himself (see Example 4).

By contrast with this, the surrounding solos by Shadow are resolute, setting out from a B pedal in the trumpet and making much use of a fateful rhythmic motif, dotted semiquaver followed by demisemiquaver

Ex. 4

(see Example 5). This motif, already introduced in Tom's opening stanzas (see Example 2), will return with magnified force to give a shuddering accompaniment to Shadow's last aria later in the scene, where the evil he is here planning for Tom falls instead upon him.

For the moment, however, Shadow is prepared to hold up the progress of the narrative and of time, just as he had previously in the Brothel scene. The duet ends, after his second B minor stanza, with the striking of a clock which he stops after nine strokes – and after Tom has anticipated the hopelessness of his situation with the words 'Too late'. It seems that Shadow is unwilling to allow his victim such a premature release from anxiety: hence his brisk switch from menace to the urbane proposition of a game, and from arioso to recitative.

Ex. 5

[musical example: Nick — "you shall slay your-self For __ for-feit is your life."; Tutti accompaniment, ♪ = 84, *ten.*, *f*, *sf*]

This recitative is quite unusual. All the others so far in the opera have been unmeasured, but here Stravinsky gives the indication crotchet = 69. Thus the tempo is to be that of the prelude, though now with a quaver rather than crotchet pulse, and so the opera is continuing at what has been established as Shadow's speed. The harpsichord for this recitative also seems suddenly more experienced. Whereas before it has concerned itself almost exclusively with simple chords, normally first inversions, now it begins in this style but goes on to introduce some variety of figures. A gentle succession of three chords, making a gesture of opening and closure, appears when Tom finds a pack of cards in his pocket, and then later, when Shadow points to the path that Tom must follow if he is unlucky, the accompaniment points also towards the 'track of cloven hooves' that Tom will notice in the ensuing duet.

None of this, however, is much preparation for the next part of the scene, where the harpsichord carries the burden of the accompaniment throughout what is a lengthy and climactic number. Stravinsky could not have found any precedent for this in Mozart or any other classical composer; it was typical only of him to hit upon a quite new possibility with the means available. It also turns out that the harpsichord is astonishingly apt at this point, not just in providing arpeggios which picturesquely suggest Shadow's shuffling of the cards, but also in giving an atmosphere that is black but brilliant, intimate yet of crucial importance.

This second duet of the scene, like the first, and like most of the other larger numbers of the opera, begins with a symmetrical arrange-

In an operatic graveyard: Act III scene 2

ment of short sections, corresponding to the first two of the three rounds of Shadow's game (one may remember here that the ballet *Jeu de cartes* had three deals). To begin with, Shadow shuffles and Tom expresses his anxiety of choice (see Example 6). The key signature here

Ex. 6

does not mean a great deal: the two hands of the keyboard player are exploring keys separated by a semitone and by an opposition of mode, chiefly F major and F sharp minor, and G major and G sharp minor. The feeling is of a musical quicksand in which Tom tries in vain to find his footing. At his very first entry (Example 6), he cannot decide between C sharp to agree with the F sharp minor of the right hand or C natural to concur with the F major of the left.

There is then a drop in the harmonic tension of the accompaniment as Shadow, in G major again, the key in which he feels himself most in control (compare the very end of Act I scene 1), reflects Tom's fears back at him. Tom thereupon thinks of Anne, whom he names to a middle C: his previous doubts have gone, and he picks on the note that has been her tonic in several previous numbers. The trap of the harpsichord's two-part invention returns, but Tom defies this to name the card as the Queen of Hearts, which Shadow accepts as correct. His following aside to the audience comes to a little, absurdly perky gavotte in A minor (see Example 7). This contributes to the impression that some

Ex. 7

kind of baroque suite is going on underneath the opera (again a parallel with *Capriccio*), with all its implications of patterned form and stylised dance. The tempo of crotchet = 112 makes this section stand out abruptly from its surroundings, taking place at Shadow's pace of quaver = 69.

The second round proceeds very much as the first, which makes the subsequent diversions from the plan all the more potent. First Shadow, in a recitative of stern warning where the principal key is E minor, reminds Tom that the next card will be his last. Tom despairs of his chances, and suddenly the crisp harpsichord is replaced for the first

In an operatic graveyard: Act III scene 2

time in the duet by a woodwind sextet folding around his words (see Example 8). The soft colour comes as something entirely new: the impression is of the score reaching forward a hand to commiserate with the leading character in his hour of greatest test.

Ex. 8

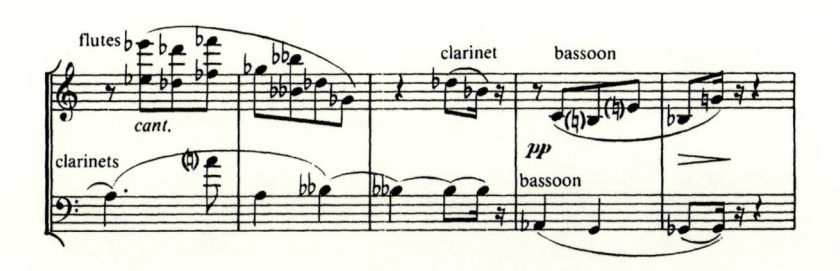

Shadow's second aside is an offbeat toccata, and then, after a further short passage of recitative enabling him to replace the Queen of Hearts in the pack, there is another halting dance, one of mutating tonality, with Tom and Shadow taking formalised duet parts as if in a number from a baroque cantata (see Example 9). The deep irony here intensifies the feeling that the next moments will be vital, and the togetherness of the participants is all illusory, for they cannot decide on the key of the piece, which slips around various flat tonalities. It is intriguing that the opening of this section should have reminded Stravinsky of the octaves in *The Nightingale* at the point in the last act where Death agrees to return the Emperor's sword and standard if only he can hear the Nightingale sing again (see Example 10).[2] Perhaps somewhere at the back of his mind, therefore, the composer was here anticipating Tom's triumph over Shadow, his grasping back of his treasure at the last moment.

88 The Rake's Progress

Ex. 9

Ex. 10

In an operatic graveyard: Act III scene 2

Following this, and once more in emphatic G major, Shadow calls on Tom to try his luck for the last time. Tom sees the hoofprints and hears Anne, singing in the now familiar tempo of quaver = 84 (circa), half the speed of her original line. The strings bounce back – another timbral shock when nearly the whole of this long duet has been accompanied by harpsichord only – and the tempo increases fourfold as Tom ecstatically welcomes the renewal brought by Love, reaching the warmth of D flat major in his last rhapsodic line (see Example 11).

Ex. 11

Shadow's subsequent aria, in the relative minor, is again in the tempo of quaver = 84, confirming a return to the 'tempo area' of the opening of the scene. The coda, however, is slower, with solo trumpet tracing a course from the pit of F flat, polar opposite of the aria's tonic, to F, dominant of the B flat major of the next and final section. It appears that the victory of the quaver = 84 'tempo area', and the seeming return to the status quo, were both unreal: when dawn rises on Tom the woodwind ritornello from the beginning of the scene does indeed come back, but at Shadow's speed of quaver = 138 (i.e. crotchet = 69, the tempo of the prelude). Furthermore, Tom now accepts Shadow's ballad tune for his verses, and even takes up the original key of B flat major from the off-stage interruptions of the Auction scene (see Example 12). He is robbed, however, of the decisively diatonic accompaniment, having instead the uncertain, melancholy woodwind, and he lingers on the mediant, where before Shadow had anchored him to the tonic. In the Auction scene the ballad tune had mad words but music that made it boldly iconoclastic: now the words are reasonable, but the setting reveals Tom's true state of mind. Everything is prepared for the following scene in Bedlam.

Ex. 12

In an operatic graveyard: Act III scene 2

is my name,

8 *Progress and return*

The paradox of drama is that we feel its actors to be independent agents while knowing them to be following a predestined course. We sympathise with Hamlet in his indecisiveness, and yet we can have no doubts, even should we be unfamiliar with the play, that all his decisions have been made for him by his creator in advance. In opera this paradox is still more sharply felt, for not only are the participants' lines laid down but even in timing and mode of delivery they have their parts prescribed, and they have too an orchestra to bind them securely to the machine of the work. To consider an opera as a work in time, therefore, is to be confronted by an artifice which transports its characters along fixed routes to fixed ends. And yet the behaviour of those characters contradicts this impression utterly. In having access to song they command a world much richer and more direct in its emotional effect than speech – there is ample proof of this in those operas where the two kinds coexist, such as *Ariadne auf Naxos* or *Die Zauberflöte* – and so they seem to exist as persons with abundant wills of their own.

It is not surprising, therefore, that the conflict between individual will and general circumstances, whether of nature or of society, should be so often at the centre of operatic drama. Monteverdi's Orpheus, Mozart's Don Juan and Berg's Lulu are all people who set out on courses that run absolutely counter to convention, and the same principle of opposition is very obviously to the fore in Wagner. So it is too in *The Rake's Progress*, where the very artificiality of the construct makes it possible for the characters to be conscious, to different degrees, of the extent to which they are embroiled in a design, the extent to which they are exercising free will.

At one extreme, Baba the Turk makes no pretence of individual freedom. She can afford to be a grotesque, and to parade herself as such without embarrassment, because she knows that she is taking part in an opera. As a performer herself, she is thoroughly at home in the world of aria and ensemble: her big D minor aria is one of the most blatantly 'operatic' moments in the work, in the sense of being extravagant and put on for display. Moreover, quite unlike Tom, for instance, she voices no doubts about belonging with her accompaniment. She has none of his uncertainty about singing in the same key as the orchestra or keeping to the orchestral metre, and her numbers are among the few in the opera where the tonality is unambiguous, the musical substance firm and coherent. Baba also has little recourse to the less artificial style of recitative, and she is the only character who has none of the secco sort.

This is especially significant. Secco recitative indicates an exit from the formal progress of the opera, an attempt by the characters to remove themselves from the highly ordered pattern which the composer has fixed for them (of course it is still the composer who pulls the strings, but the impression is of greatly enlarged freedom). Stravinsky was the first composer since the early nineteenth century to use simple recitative in the conventional manner, Britten's usage in *The Rape of Lucretia* being much more personal to him, and so *The Rake's Progress* provides its characters with avenues of escape that have long lain unused. As already mentioned, Baba will have none of them, but to Shadow they are a gift. Except in the first and last scenes, and excepting also two extremely short episodes in the Auction scene, it is always Nick who initiates dry recitative: he does so three times in Act I scene 1, and once each time in Act I scene 2, Act II scene 1, Act II scene 3 and Act III scene 2, these being all the scenes in which he appears. Against this, passages of simple recitative are started once by the Keeper of the Madhouse, once by Trulove in each of the outermost scenes (his recitatives are the first and last in the whole opera) and twice briefly by Sellem.

The Keeper is a character too insignificant to make much impression on the audience. Sellem uses dry recitative because he is prepared to employ any trick in the book. Trulove adopts it with no qualms, and he even introduces this genre, because he is a character belonging wholly in the world of eighteenth-century opera, though he does not appear to share Baba's realisation of participating in a stage event: only Baba, as the Epilogue will show, knows that all the world is theatre.

Shadow's case is different. The instances of his initiating simple recitative are more numerous and more widely spaced in the opera. He moves between the formality of the accompanied number and the informality of dry recitative with ease, and it seems entirely possible, because of this ease, that he alone of the characters could move just as readily between the stage and the wider world. Only he picks up crucial props outside – the broadsheet in Act II scene 1, the fantastic machine in

Act II scene 3 — which suggests that only he can venture beyond the theatre, and when he is absent from the stage, as he is for example in Act II scene 2, it is tempting to imagine him at work in the world. We even seem to hear him there, with Tom now decisively his tool, in the Auction scene, and again the Epilogue contains a clue in warning the audience to beware of him.

Yet this is surely to accept Shadow at his own valuation. He believes himself to be in control of the opera, demonstrating this by the freedom with which he departs from it, but in fact we know that this is not so, that the only organisers of the proceedings are the composer and his librettists. Until the end Shadow never has any doubts about his own powers, is even so sure of himself as to rely on the most obvious trickery (Act II scene 3) or tease Tom with possibilities of salvation (Act III scene 2). When the game goes against him and he is drawn down to Hell, no-one is more surprised than himself: his B flat minor aria is the most forceful number in the Graveyard scene and the only one of Shadow's contributions in which he is caught without his irony, the only one too in which he loses the confidence of the major mode. Right up to this point he sees himself as master.

Tom is never so sure: indeed, his character is all inconsistency and doubt. This appears from the first, for his first-scene aria 'Since it is not by merit' expounds his view that he is a puppet of fate while also having him assume, most humanly, that fate will be on his side, that though will-less he will have his wishes granted. Shadow then encourages him to believe that he can make his own decisions and live by them, that he is a free agent, but he is never really convinced of this. He experiments by removing himself tonally from his accompaniment, with the equivocations particularly invasive in 'Vary the song' and the duet at the beginning of the Graveyard scene, as has been mentioned. He also essays freedom by decorating his line. 'Since it is not by merit' and its preceding orchestral recitative are largely syllabic, as if he were here happy to take the notes dealt him by Fortune, but thereafter he introduces a variety of curlicues to give the superficial impression that he is making some choices of his own (by contrast, Shadow's line is plain, because he has no need to convince himself, and Baba's accepts the ornate as merely conventional). Tom's hankering after a proof of freedom in ornamentation continues even in the Bedlam scene, and indeed reaches an extreme in his highly elaborate song of farewell 'My heart breaks', where he at last makes a direct claim on the kinship with Monteverdi's Orpheus promised right from the opening of the opera.

But Tom's pretended independence is made quite plainly puny, since his embellishments do not evince personal will at all but rather a wavering and doubt about the existence of that will. If he has proved his liberation from prostration before Fortune, if he has demonstrated too his freedom from the dictates of social pressure and personal taste, he has yet remained subject to Shadow. His final choice, and his only completely independent one, is to destroy Shadow, but in doing this he is also destroying a part of himself, for by this stage, after the ballad tune, the identification of servant and master has become quite clear, and so Shadow's departure leaves him witless.

Up to this point Tom is the only character who has gained any knowledge of what is going on, for at least uncertainty has replaced his naive self-belief of the beginning; which is why the opera can be said to be about his progress. Baba knows she is in an opera and exults in the fact. Shadow thinks he is in a construction to which he alone has the key, and his discovery that this is not so is sudden, not progressive. Trulove and Anne believe themselves to be within the real world, knowing no other, and they behave accordingly. Their emotions feel genuine, and when the opera is over they are left exactly as they were at the start. One may well then feel cheated that they should appear in the Epilogue, implying that all their previous honesty has been deceit, that they knew all along that they were only characters in an opera, whereas Baba and Shadow had never made any pretence of behaving realistically, and Tom had begun to realise he was in an opera just before he was struck insane. At this point he made the decision to break with realism and call upon Anne to help him, knowing her to be a soprano no further away than the wings.

It is evident that an opera dealing thus with the self-awareness of its creatures could be written only at a late stage in the history of the art, because it could achieve its ends only by returning to that history. And indeed this late period in operatic composition almost imposes self-consciousness. The failure of a great many twentieth-century operas is due to the fact that the audience is considerably more sophisticated than the persons exhibited on stage. An opera in our age can work only if its characters are musically and dramatically new to the art, and probably therefore extraordinary beings (Salome, Wozzeck, Moses), or if they recognise in some measure that they are contained in an opera, which will require them to look back over the traditions of the genre (as in *The Rake's Progress*, or *Capriccio*, or Berio's *Opera*).

Thus neoclassicism in *The Rake's Progress* is not a sign of weakness or satirical intent (or at least not only that) but a manner essential to the meaning of the work. Stravinsky had always spoken, or been made to speak, as if neoclassicism were a necessary aesthetic, as if all would be well if only artists would abide by the rules of bygone ages: Roland-Manuel has him quoting Verdi to this effect at the end of the second lecture in the *Poetics of Music*, saying: 'Let us return to old times, and that will be progress.'[1] But in the field of opera neoclassicism had not scored many successes. Hindemith's most combatively neoclassical opera, the first version of *Cardillac* (1926), took pride in the fact that it was not an opera at all but a concert with simultaneous play, and Busoni's *Arlecchino* and *Turandot* (both 1917), perhaps the first neoclassical operas, were deliberately constructed as puppet dramas, so that there was an accord between musical and theatrical stylisation. And the same may be said of Stravinsky's own *Mavra*, which, it will be recalled, was his last true opera before *The Rake's Progress*, his last attempt to tell a theatrical story without the obvious distancing effect of dance narration.

The Rake's Progress uses and exploits neoclassicism very much more thoroughly and acutely, takes the appurtenances of traditional opera to create its décor, the very world of its existence. Most obviously is the revival of the harpsichord a 'return to old times'. It was an instrument that Stravinsky had used before only in the abortive orchestral version of *The Wedding*, and that he suddenly now elevated to the place it held in the eighteenth century (there appears to be no earlier example of the operatic use of the harpsichord in the twentieth century — except the very different one of *Capriccio*). But apart from this resurrected convention, there are clear debts to Mozart in the scale of the music, the shape of its numbers (though Stravinsky has no place for the extended finales of *Don Giovanni* and *Le nozze di Figaro*) and even the material of particular items: Deryck Cooke draws attention to the relation between Anne's cabaletta 'I go to him' and the Rondo in D, K.382, and to that between the chorus 'How sad a song' and the quintet 'Di scrivermi' from *Così fan tutte*.[2] But to criticise Stravinsky, as Cooke does, for a 'misunderstanding of 18th-century constructive principles' is surely to miss the point, for Stravinsky was not seeking to make a work in perfect classical style, a work that could be mistaken for the creation of one of Mozart's contemporaries if not of Mozart himself. Rather he needed the period references, even quite specific references, to make it clear that his characters were going through the motions of an eighteenth-century opera. He needed too his own twists to show that some of them are sometimes aware of this, and that he certainly is even when they are not.

Another of Cooke's examples can be used to demonstrate how and why this happens. Cooke quotes part of Anne's line from the trio of Act II scene 2 (see Example 13) and points out rightly that it contains a Mozartian cadential formula (beginning of the second bar) which Stravinsky 'uses in the middle of his melodic line' and then 'omits the

Ex. 13

obligatory ending, and reaches no cadence at all'. This is, however, not mere wilfulness or ignorance. The disappointment of hopes for a conventional cadence – followed by the abrupt stopping of the music at no point of rest – heightens the poignancy of Anne's (and, indeed, Tom's) lament here over the conflict between love on the one hand and happiness in the expression of feeling on the other. Nor is it, surely, by accident that Stravinsky writes inconclusive music for the word 'never'.

As has already become apparent, the references in *The Rake's Progress* are by no means limited to Mozart or even to the eighteenth century. Monteverdi's *Orfeo* is invoked by the fanfare Prelude to the first scene, by the pastoral tone of the opening, by the progress of the hero from a natural to a regimented world (Hades/London) and back again, transfigured by experience, and by the elaborate style of Tom's last song. Turning to the nineteenth century, Stravinsky himself acknowledged a debt to the trumpet solo at the start of Act II of *Don Pasquale*,[3] presumably thinking of the solo for the same instrument in the introduction to Act II scene 2 of his own opera, in the identical key of C minor, and Baba obviously belongs in the world of Verdi rather than Mozart. Thus, without explicitly parodying particular originals except on rare occasions, Stravinsky fills his operas with the memory of others, just as Berg does in *Lulu*. The difference is that Berg's reminiscences are living and organically contained within the body of his work, exactly as Lulu's pursuers are very much alive, whereas Stravinsky makes an exhibit of what is derivative in his score: like Baba, he has collected about him a museumful of curios whose provenances and functions are not important.

Apart from returning thus over the operatic repertory, *The Rake's Progress* is also a personal return. During the time of its composition Stravinsky was in the process of making revised versions of earlier works so that they could be newly copyrighted by Boosey & Hawkes: between 1947 and 1951 he was at work on *The Rite of Spring*, the *Symphonies of Wind Instruments*, *Oedipus rex*, *Apollo*, the *Symphony of Psalms*, *Perséphone* and several other works of the previous four decades. Obviously it is not easy to be sure that recollections of other works in *The Rake's Progress* are genuine recollections, whether conscious or not, rather than simply stylistic traits, but we have the composer's sanction for noting two correspondences: that with *The Nightingale* mentioned in the previous chapter, and the section of iambic dance for strings at Fig. 212 in Act II, which he described as 'purely Apollonian, and I do not mean the "philosophy", but the notes'. Apollonian in the sense of looking back to *Apollo*.

Moreover, the Faustian and cyclical aspects of the narrative have many parallels among Stravinsky's earlier works, again going back as far as *The Nightingale*, where the Emperor allows the mechanical bird (compare the stones-to-bread machine in *The Rake*) to usurp the place of the real one, whose departure thereupon threatens his life. *Histoire du soldat* is much more fully a Faust story, while the cycle of the seasons, and in particular the potency of spring as a renewal through death, is an aspect of such otherwise dissimilar works as *The Rite of Spring* and *Perséphone*. There are even connections with the farmyard entertainment *Baize*, which is again a cyclical piece, and where the appearances of the Fox are signalled by a cimbalom arpeggio not dissimilar to those in the harpsichord that herald Shadow: both characters are tempters eventually confounded.

It becomes clear that in *The Rake's Progress*, far from withdrawing into some rococo wonderland, Stravinsky was dealing with musical and dramatic themes that had always mattered to him closely. The seasonal cycle, giving the illusion that new beginnings are always possible, is contained in the wheel of the opera, though here when spring returns, at the end of the Graveyard scene, Tom is mad, and the only people left untouched are those for whom time has no meaning, either because they have been insane all along (the Bedlam inmates) or else because for one reason or another they accept the conventions of the opera as a vehicle of return (Baba, Anne, Trulove), for they know that in successive

Progress and return

performances the wheel will continue to turn, that each playing of the Bedlam scene is only the prelude to the next presentation of the pastoral.

Only those who risk the quest for knowledge and experience, who try like Tom to break out of the circle, can be harmed by the progress of the clock. And hence the link between the cyclical and the Faustian strains in Stravinsky's theatre, hence the link too between progress and return. The cycles of the natural world — including not only the seasonal but also the lunar and diurnal cycles — make us suppose subconsciously that repetition is a truth of our lives, that every day, every month, every year is a fresh start, with the slate wiped clean. Shadow, representing subconscious levels in the dual central character, is wholly of this opinion, and for him time is of no account: he can turn the clock back or stop it at will. With our conscious minds, however, we know that there is no going back. Like Tom, we are caught in an ineluctable progress to death. And so Tom, as human consciousness, is appalled by the passing of time: 'Too late' is his cry at moments of high anxiety in the Brothel and Graveyard scenes.

The simultaneous presentation of progress and return is something possible only in music, and most particularly in Stravinsky's non-developing style, where the music appears to exist outside time while at the same time it measures time most precisely. Much of this effect is owed to Stravinsky's tonality. Often the key of a passage is not inherent in the music but exists instead as a background perspective, established by means of a pedal or an arpeggio ostinato, against which the more foreground features are placed, or rather displaced. This is especially clear in much of Tom's music, where the common antagonism of tonic and dominant is very open (in, for example, 'Since it is not by merit' or 'Love, too frequently betrayed'). Often the opposition of tonalities is made more exquisite by modal inflections, giving a distinctively English flavour that suggests Stravinsky's models included not only Monteverdi, Mozart, Donizetti and Verdi but also Purcell and indeed Britten. In his mad song at the end of the Graveyard scene (Example 12), for instance, Tom is gently dissociated from the B flat pedal by his adoption of Phrygian D minor.

The opera's device of putting tonality in the background is also apparent in the formal structuring of individual numbers, where, as has often been remarked, Stravinsky does not modulate but rather slips from one key into another. This is most disconcerting in the Graveyard scene, with its opening exchanges of G minor and G major or its insidious counterposing of unrelated keys in the card game; but it is a feature of the opera throughout. In most cases the middle sections of ternary arias and ensembles are in a different key from the outer parts, but the changes are sudden or proceed scale-wise rather than in accordance with 'correct' principles. Tonality is not a language which the music breathes, but rather a means of creating directional pulls which it may go along with, resist or change without warning. And it is the same here as it is in the use of operatic references, that the work returns to past conventions not to inhabit them but to use them in ways of its own. Such an attitude could only be taken by a composer for whom both tonality and opera were dead: *The Rake's Progress* is an opera created within the ruins of a finished tradition.

As such, it is, simply by its existence, a powerful image of the message that whatever the cycles of clocks, seasons and planets may indicate, there is no return in human affairs. Second chances can be granted only by God, and it is Tom's tragedy that he fails to recognise this. Anne gives him the hint in her words at the moment of his highest danger – 'A Love / that is sworn before thee can plunder Hell of its prey' – but this makes him look to human rather than to divine love. On the one occasion when he does use the word 'God', in his despair before the third round of the Graveyard game, he does not notice that the orchestra comes forward to enclose him and encourage him, and the moment is lost. He has also been guilty of the highest blasphemy in bidding for Christ's place through his supposed invention of the stones-to-bread machine, putting his faith in objects in the manner that Sellem will later echo.

By contrast, Anne and Trulove recognise that God is to be thanked for good fortune (quartet in Act I scene 1: simultaneously Tom and Shadow are thanking each other and blind chance), though Trulove takes the Calvinist line that everything is ordained by God (Act III scene 3) whereas Anne sees the possibility of change being wrought through prayer (Act I scene 3 and Act II scene 2). This adds another level to the opera's argument between will and destiny, but the important thing is that both Anne and Trulove believe. By putting themselves in the hands of God, who exists beyond time, they liberate themselves from the demands of the subconscious, similarly existing beyond time, and so they cannot fall prey to their Shadows.

God, it appears, is served only by the timeless. After finishing *The Rake's Progress* Stravinsky took up an anonymous modal style in his Cantata, set to anonymous texts. There was to be no more toying with Mozart or others, no more neoclassicism. But then the opera tells us that musical return had always depended precisely on its impossibility: the recapitulation is and is not the exposition.

Notes

2 The makers and their work

1. Igor Stravinsky and Robert Craft, *Memories and Commentaries* (New York, Doubleday, 1960; London, Faber, 1960), p. 131.
2. *The Daily Mail*, 13 February 1913.
3. 'Stravinsky, Roland-Manuel and the *Poetics of Music*', *The Stravinsky Festival: Special Supplement to the 1979 Programme* (xeroxed sheets, n.p., n.d.)
4. Ibid. p. 9.
5. Ibid. p. 9.
6. Stravinsky and Craft, *Memories and Commentaries*, p. 154.
7. Vera Stravinsky and Robert Craft, *Stravinsky in Pictures and Documents* (New York, Simon & Schuster, 1978; London, Hutchinson, 1979), p. 396; see also pp. 396–415 for a detailed chronology of the opera's genesis.
8. Stravinsky and Craft, *Memories and Commentaries*, p. 154.
9. See Donald Mitchell, *Britten and Auden in the Thirties: the Year 1936* (London, Faber, 1981).
10. Stravinsky and Craft, *Memories and Commentaries*, p. 154.
11. Stravinsky and Craft, *Stravinsky in Pictures*, p. 396.
12. Robert Craft, ed., *Stravinsky: Selected Correspondence* (London, Faber, and University of California Press, at press).
13. Igor Stravinsky, *Poetics of Music* (Cambridge, Massachusetts, Harvard University Press, 1970), pp. 80–1.
14. Stravinsky and Craft, *Stravinsky in Pictures*, p. 397.
15. Charles Osborne, *W.H. Auden* (London, Eyre Methuen, 1979), pp. 229–30.
16. Craft, ed., *Stravinsky: Selected Correspondence*.
17. Stravinsky and Craft, *Stravinsky in Pictures*, p. 397.
18. Stravinsky and Craft, *Memories and Commentaries*, pp. 167–76.
19. Craft, ed., *Stravinsky: Selected Correspondence*.
20. Stravinsky and Craft, *Stravinsky in Pictures*, pp. 409–10.
21. W. H. Auden, *The Dyer's Hand* (London, Faber, 1963), p. 110.
22. Craft, ed., *Stravinsky: Selected Correspondence*.
23. See above, pp. 3–4.
24. Stravinsky and Craft, *Memories and Commentaries*, p. 157.
25. Stravinsky and Craft, *Stravinsky in Pictures*, p. 398.
26. Ibid. p. 398.

Notes to pp. 14–51

27 Craft, ed., *Stravinsky: Selected Correspondence.*
28 Ibid.
29 Stravinsky and Craft, *Stravinsky in Pictures*, p. 650.
30 Ibid. p. 401.
31 Ibid. p. 401.
32 Ibid. p. 401.
33 Ibid. p. 402.
34 'Some Reflections on Opera as a Medium', *Tempo*, 20 (1951), pp. 6–10; reprinted as 'Notes on Music and Opera' in *The Dyer's Hand*, pp. 465–74.
35 Craft, ed., *Stravinsky: Selected Correspondence.*
36 Information from Robert Craft.
37 Published in *Botteghe oscure*, 12 (1953), 164–210.
38 Stravinsky and Craft, *Stravinsky in Pictures*, pp. 204–5.
39 Igor Stravinsky and Robert Craft, *Themes and Episodes* (New York, Knopf, 1966), p. 23.
40 For fuller details see the articles on Auden and Kallman in *The New Grove*.

3 A note on the sketches and the two versions of the libretto

1 Other sketches and a page from Stravinsky's typescript of the libretto are reproduced in Stravinsky and Craft, *Stravinsky in Pictures*, Plates 13–14, and a page of the libretto in Auden's rough draft appears in Eric Walter White, *Stravinsky: the Composer and his Works* (London, Faber, 1966, second edition 1979), p. 454.

5 Performance history

1 Stravinsky and Craft, *Stravinsky in Pictures*, p. 404.
2 Ibid. p. 406.
3 Ibid. p. 407.
4 Craft, ed., *Stravinsky: Selected Correspondence.*
5 Stravinsky and Craft, *Stravinsky in Pictures*, p. 409.
6 Ibid. p. 402.
7 Ibid. p. 410.
8 '*The Rake's Progress* in Venice', published in the programme for the 1953 Boston University Opera Workshop production, and partly reprinted in White, *Stravinsky*, p. 467.
9 '*The Rake's Progress*: "La prima assoluta"', in Stravinsky and Craft, *Themes and Episodes*, pp. 51–4; reprinted in Stravinsky, *Themes and Conclusions* (London, Faber, 1972), pp. 55–7.
10 'Strawinsky and *The Rake's Progress*', *Opera*, 2 (1951), 610–18.
11 Stravinsky and Craft, *Stravinsky in Pictures*, p. 413.
12 'Stravinsky's Opera', *Music and Letters*, 33 (1952), 1–9.
13 Stravinsky and Craft, *Stravinsky in Pictures*, p. 416.
14 Ibid. p. 419.
15 Robert Craft, *Stravinsky: the Chronicle of a Friendship* (New York, Knopf, 1972; London, Gollancz, 1972), p. 114.
16 Ibid. p. 116.

Notes to pp. 51–97

17 Ibid. p. 116.
18 Ibid. p. 114.
19 Stravinsky and Craft, *Stravinsky in Pictures*, p. 462.
20 Craft, *Stravinsky: the Chronicle of a Friendship*, p. 114.
21 Ibid. p. 116.
22 Stravinsky and Craft, *Stravinsky in Pictures*, p. 462.
23 Ibid. p. 461.
24 Craft, *Stravinsky: the Chronicle of a Friendship*, p. 117.
25 Ibid. pp. 354–5.
26 Sketch reproduced in David Hockney, *David Hockney* (London, Thames & Hudson, 1978), p. 284.
27 *The Musical Times*, 120 (1979), 669.

6 Some thoughts on the libretto

1 See above, p. 2.

7 In an operatic graveyard: Act III scene 2

1 Stravinsky and Craft, *Stravinsky in Pictures*, p. 406.
2 Igor Stravinsky and Robert Craft, *Dialogues and a Diary* (New York, Doubleday, 1913; London, Faber, 1968), p. 34.

8 Progress and return

1 Stravinsky, *Poetics of Music*, pp. 58–9.
2 'The Rake and the 18th Century', *The Musical Times*, 103 (1962), 20–3.
3 Stravinsky and Craft, *Dialogues and a Diary*, p. 34.

Bibliography

i. The opera

Full score (London, Boosey & Hawkes, 1951)
Vocal score by Leopold Spinner (London, Boosey & Hawkes, 1951)
Libretto in English (London, Boosey & Hawkes, 1951)
Libretto in French translation by André de Badet, as *Le libertin* (London, Boosey & Hawkes, 1951)
Libretto in German translation by Fritz Schroeder, as *Der Wüstling* (London, Boosey & Hawkes, 1951)
Libretto in Italian translation by Rinaldo Küfferle, as *Carriera d'un libertino* (London, Boosey & Hawkes, 1951)
The manuscript full and vocal scores are held by the University of Southern California; other material, including sketches and typescripts, is the property of the Stravinsky Estate.

ii. On the opera

W. H. Auden, *The Dyer's Hand* (London, Faber, 1963)
    'Some Reflections on Opera as a Medium', *Tempo*, 20 (1951), 6–10; reprinted as 'Notes on Music and Opera' in *The Dyer's Hand*, pp. 465–74
Deryck Cooke, '*The Rake* and the 18th Century', *The Musical Times*, 103 (1962), 20–3
Robert Craft, '*The Rake's Progress* in Venice', published in the programme for the 1953 Boston University Opera Workshop production, and partly reprinted in Eric Walter White, *Stravinsky: the Composer and his Works* (London, Faber, second edition 1979)
    'Reflections on "The Rake's Progress"', *The Score*, 9 (1954), 24–30
    Stravinsky: the Chronicle of a Friendship (New York, Knopf, 1972; London, Gollancz, 1972)
    'Stravinsky, Roland-Manuel and the *Poetics of Music*', *The Stravinsky Festival: Special Supplement to the 1979 Programme* (xeroxed sheets, n.p., n.d.)
    ed., *Stravinsky: Selected Correspondence* (London, Faber, and University of California Press, at press)
Guida a 'The Rake's Progress' (Venice, 1951)
Lord Harewood, 'Strawinsky and *The Rake's Progress*', *Opera*, 2 (1951), 610–18.

Bibliography

David Hockney, *David Hockney* (London, Thames & Hudson, 1978)
Joseph Kerman, 'Opera à la mode', *The Hudson Review*, 6:4 (1953); reprinted in *Opera*, 5 (1954), 411–15 and 491–5; incorporated with some changes in *Opera as Drama* (New York, Knopf, 1956)
Colin Mason, 'Stravinsky's Opera', *Music and Letters*, 33 (1952), 1–9
Donald Mitchell, *Britten and Auden in the Thirties: the Year 1936* (London, Faber, 1981)
Charles Osborne, *W.H. Auden* (London, Eyre Methuen, 1979)
Igor Stravinsky, *Poetics of Music* (Cambridge, Massachusetts, Harvard University Press, 1970)
    'The Rake's Progress', in Igor Stravinsky and Robert Craft, *Memories and Commentaries*, pp. 154–76
    Themes and Conclusions (London, Faber, 1972)
Igor Stravinsky and Robert Craft, *Dialogues and a Diary* (New York, Doubleday, 1963; London, Faber, 1968)
    Memories and Commentaries (New York, Doubleday, 1960; London, Faber, 1960)
    Themes and Episodes (New York, Knopf, 1966)
Vera Stravinsky, '*The Rake's Progress*: "La prima assoluta"', in Igor Stravinsky and Robert Craft, *Themes and Episodes* (New York, Knopf, 1966), pp. 51–4
Vera Stravinsky and Robert Craft, *Stravinsky in Pictures and Documents* (London, Hutchinson, 1979), especially pp. 396–415
Eric Walter White, *Stravinsky: the Composer and his Works* (London, Faber, second edition 1979)

Discography
BY MALCOLM WALKER

A Anne Trulove; *T* Tom Rakewell; *N* Nick Shadow; *B* Baba the Turk; *Tr* Trulove; *S* Sellem the auctioneer; *MG* Mother Goose; *K* Keeper of the Madhouse

1953   Gueden *A*; Conley *T*; Harrell *N*; Thebom *B*; Scott *Tr*; Franke *S*; Lipton *MG*; Davidson *K*/Metropolitan Opera Chorus and Orch/ Stravinsky
                              Philips ⓜ ABL3055—7
                              CBS (US) ⓜ SL125

1964   Raskin *A*; Young *T*; Reardon *N*; Sarfaty *B*; Garrard *Tr*; Miller *S*; Manning *MG*; Tracey *K*/Sadler's Wells Opera Chorus, RPO/ Stravinsky
                              CBS (UK) 77304
                              (US) M3S-710

Excerpts
1967   (live performance — Salle Wilfred Pelletier, Montreal; in Swedish); Act II Scene 3; Ulfung *T*; Ericson *B*/Royal Opera Orch, Stockholm/Varviso
                              EMI (Sweden) 7C 153 35350—8

1972   Anne's aria and cabaletta (in Swedish); Hallin *A*/Norrköping SO/Björlin
                              EMI (Sweden) 4E 061 34616

Index

Allen, Betty 54
Andersen, Hans Christian 5
Ariè, Rafael 49
Armistead, Horace 50
Arundell, Dennis 50
Auden, Wystan Hugh *passim*
  Ascent of F6, The 10
  Bassarids, The 17
  Delia 16
  Elegy for Young Lovers 17
  Love's Labour's Lost 17
  Moralities 17
  Night Mail 10
  Paul Bunyan 12

Balanchine, George 50
Bellini, Vincenzo 12
Berg, Alban 2, 63
  Lulu 92, 97
  Wozzeck 63, 67, 95
Bergling, Berger 51
Bergman, Ingmar 51–4
Berio, Luciano 95
Berlioz, Hector 16, 63
Berman, Eugene 49
Boito, Arrigo 4
Boulanger, Nadia 7
Bowen, Kenneth 51
Britten, Benjamin 10, 12, 99
  Rape of Lucretia, The 93
Browning, Robert 62
Busoni, Ferruccio 96
Byam Shaw, Glen 54

Caldwell, Sarah 50, 56
Cavalcanti, Guido 70
Cézanne, Paul 62

Chávez, Carlos 17
Cluytens, André 50
Cocteau, Jean 61
Colciaghi, Ebe 49
Conley, Eugene 50, 51, 106
Cooke, Deryck 96-7
Cox, John 56
Craft, Robert 7, 14, 16, 49, 50, 51, 54, 56, 74
Cuenod, Hugues 49

Dante Aligheri 70
Davies, Peter Maxwell 73
Davis, Colin 54, 56
Debussy, Claude 5
Dickens, Charles 62, 65
Diderot, Denis 65
Dittersdorf, Karl Ditters von 17
Donath, Helen 56
Donizetti, Gaetano 12, 99
  Don Pasquale 97
Dostoevsky, Fyodor 69
Driscoll, Loren 51
Dryden, John 4
Dyagilev, Sergey 5, 6, 48

Ebert, Carl 48, 49, 50, 54
Ebert, Peter 56
Eliot, Thomas Stearns 60, 61, 62, 63, 70
Ellis, Rosalind 56
Elmo, Cloè 49

Firth, Tazeena 56

Gibson, Alexander 56
Gielen, Michael 51

Index

Glinka, Mikhail 6
Gluck, Christoph Willibald 2
Goeke, Leo 56
Golding, William 67
Gomez, Jill 56
Gordon, Gavin 8
Gramm, Donald 56
Gueden, Hilde 50, 106

Haitink, Bernard 56
Hallin, Margareta 51, 106
Harewood, Lord 49
Harrell, Mack 50, 106
Harrison, Rex 8
Hawkes, Ralph 10, 15
Hayter, Raymond 51
Hedeby, Kerstin 51
Henze, Hans Werner 17
Herincx, Raimund 54
Hindemith, Paul 96
Hines, Jerome 50
Hockney, David 56-9
Hofmannsthal, Hugo von 4
Hogarth, William 8, 9, 10, 11, 12, 13, 54, 56, 65
Huxley, Aldous 8

Isherwood, Christopher 10

Johnson, Patricia 56
Johnson, Samuel 3, 65

Kafka, Franz 60
Kallman, Chester *passim*
 Visitors, The 17
 see Auden for collaborative works
Kendall, Raymond 48
Kierkegaard, Søren 69
Kraus, Otakar 49, 51

Lancaster, Osbert 50
Leinsdorf, Erich 51
Leitner, Ferdinand 49
Lewis, Richard 50
Lovett, Leon 51

Magee, Bryan 57
Mann, Thomas 60

Markevich, Igor 49
Mason, Colin 50
Mendelssohn, Felix 16
Meneaugh, Michael 56
Menkes, Emanuel 49
Menotti, Gian Carlo 48, 54
Merriman, Nan 50
Meyer, Kerstin 51
Mitusov, Stepan 5
Monteverdi, Claudio 99
 Orfeo 64, 72, 94, 97
Morison, Elsie 50, 54
Moshinsky, Elijah 56
Mozart, Wolfgang Amadeus 3, 5, 10, 12, 17, 48, 77, 96-7, 99, 100
 Così fan tutte 10, 12, 50, 67, 96
 Don Giovanni 10, 64, 92, 96
 Nozze di Figaro, Le 10, 96
 Rondo in D, K.382 96
 Zauberflöte, Die 10, 92
Musy, Louis 50

Nabokov, Nicholas 17, 48
Nietzsche, Friedrich 69

O'Brien, Timothy 56

Pergolesi, Giovanni Battista 6, 12
Picasso, Pablo 62
Picchi, Mirto 49
Piper, John 49
Potter, Peter 51
Poussin, François 57
Puccini, Giacomo 56
Purcell, Henry 4, 99
Pushkin, Aleksandr 6

Ramuz, C.F. 6, 7
Raskin, Judith 54, 106
Ratto, Gianni 49
Reardon, John 54
Reiner, Fritz 50
Rimsky-Korsakov, Nikolay 5, 6
Robson, Ann 54
Roland-Manuel 7, 10, 96
Rossini, Gioacchino 16
Rounseville, Robert 49

Index

Sacher, Paul 50
Sade, Marquis de 65, 66, 68
Saedén, Erik 51
Sarfaty, Regina 54, 106
Schoenberg, Arnold 50, 67, 73
  Moses und Aron 95
Schwarzkopf, Elisabeth 49
Shakespeare, William 64, 65
Strauss, Richard 4, 5
  Ariadne auf Naxos 92
  Capriccio 77, 86, 95, 96
  Salome 95
Stravinsky, Igor *passim*
  Abraham and Isaac 60
  Agon 16
  Apollo 13, 98
  Babel 7
  Bayka (Baize) 6, 61, 98
  Cantata 16
  Circus Polka 8
  Elegy for J.F.K. 16
  Flood, The 16-17
  Histoire du soldat 6, 10, 17, 61, 98
  In memoriam Dylan Thomas 16
  Jeu de cartes 85
  Mass 7
  Mavra 6, 7, 10, 96
  Oedipus rex 5, 7, 10, 36, 60, 61, 62, 63, 98
  Orpheus 8, 10, 13, 77
  Perséphone 5, 7, 10, 13, 98
  Petrushka 5
  Piano Sonata 5, 48
  Poetics of Music 7, 8, 10
  Pulcinella 6, 12
  Solovey (The Nightingale) 5, 6, 7, 87-8
  Svadebka (The Wedding) 6, 10, 60, 61, 62, 64, 68, 75, 96
  Symphonies of Wind Instruments 98
  Symphony in C 5
  Symphony in Three Movements 8
  Symphony of Psalms 7, 54, 98
  Vesna svyashchennaya (The Rite of Spring) 5, 60, 98
  Zhar-ptitsa (The Firebird) 5
Stravinsky, Vera 49

Tangeman, Nell 49
Tchaikovsky, Pyotr 6, 62
Tear, Robert 56
Thebom, Blanche 50, 106
Thomas, Dylan 16
Tourel, Jennie 49
Trowell, Brian 51

Ulfung, Ragnar 51, 106

Valois, Ninette de 8
Verdi, Giuseppe 4, 12, 62, 63, 77, 96, 97, 99
  Ballo in maschera, Un 3
  Rigoletto 3

Wagner, Richard 2, 5, 7, 12, 63, 66, 92
  Tristan und Isolde 63, 65, 67
Wallenstein, Alfred 50
Weber, Carl Maria von 12
Webster, David 48, 56
Weill, Kurt 17

Yeats, William Butler 60
Young, Alexander 54, 55, 56, 106

Printed in the United Kingdom
by Lightning Source UK Ltd.
122795UK00001B/102/A